How to deliver
OUTSTANDING
corporate events

How to deliver
OUTSTANDING
corporate events

*A practical, step-by-step guide to
designing, planning and delivering
successful corporate events*

CHRIS POWELL
The Event Expert

ISBN: 978-1-4834-0150-8 (sc)
ISBN: 978-1-4834-0149-2 (e)

Lulu Publishing Services rev. date: 07/03/2013

Keynote

The complete **'how to'** guide to designing,
planning and delivering exciting, engaging
and rewarding corporate events

CONTENTS

ABOUT THE AUTHOR

Chris Powell, founder of The Event Expert, has been designing, planning and delivering events for the past 20 years. He has been a local authority event manager and director of a range of events, including exhibitions, food and beer festivals, press launches, music, arts and sports events and conferences, as well as a freelance event manager and coach helping a variety of organizations to deliver their events. Chris specializes in providing his clients with a full event management service, from conception to completion and everything in between.

As an event management trainer and lecturer, Chris is engaged by a range of organizations to deliver a variety of event management training courses. He trains and mentors people at all levels, from first-time event organizers and students right through to experienced event professionals.

With some 500 events completed with flying colours and over 2,000 event managers trained, Chris knows a thing or two about how to deliver successful events. His experience covers the full range of corporate events, such as showcase-style events, internal events and milestone events to name just a few. He has handled smaller-scale local events as well as major events with audiences numbering in their thousands. Over the years, he has, of course, also attended hundreds of business events. So Chris knows what works—and what works well.

My events story: a message from the author

So where did it all begin for me? As a young man, I had aspirations of being a sportsman. However, I was not good enough. I moved briefly into sports centre management, which I did not enjoy. After that, I had five very enjoyable years as a Sports Development Officer and, in January 1994, I was seconded to work on an event. As it happened, it was not just any event. I was being asked to help run the 15-mile Basingstoke stage of the Tour de France—the world's largest annual sporting event.

What did I know about events at that time? Nothing! I had run a few coaching courses. In those days, trying to find suitably experienced events people to talk to was not easy, nor was tracking down useful information. The internet was but an idea. To cut a long story short, the Basingstoke stage of the event was a huge success. We somehow managed to survive but not without many sleepless nights.

This experience taught me that, actually, we could all be great event planners. I believe opportunities to practise event management are always coming along: you just have to look for them and, when you find them, say "yes" to them.

I do, of course, accept that the somewhat pressured environment of event planning is not for everyone. My advice, if you think the world of events is for you, is that you should be ready to step outside your comfort zone. You will need to become a continuous learner and an event groupie (go to lots of events). You should also seek out good advice and have a healthy dose of belief and determination. While event management will throw up the odd challenge or three, it is immensely rewarding and I would not want to do anything else.

I for one have always passionately believed in the value, importance and tremendous impact that great events can have in our business and private lives, and so I have always been happy to help organizations and individuals deliver events of which they can be proud.

So my reason for writing this book—my cause, so to speak—is to help all of you, who often have no formal event qualification or experience to develop the confidence or skills to plan your own successful events. This book is all about what I do every day, which is designing, planning and delivering events. I will share with you my proven 8-Step Event Planning Process and everything I know about the "how to" of becoming a great corporate event planner. I do hope you find my book useful.

Chris
The Event Expert
www.theeventexpert.co.uk

CHAPTER 1

INTRODUCTION: WELCOME TO THE WORLD OF CORPORATE EVENT PLANNING

Events are a tried and tested method for businesses, associations and public bodies to reach and engage with their audiences. Events bring a variety of benefits not only to the host organizations but also to those who participate in and attend them. They can perform a wide variety of functions and are used by a range of organizations to great effect. With today's corporate event attendee always expecting a high-quality experience, creating that memorable and ultimately rewarding event is no easy task! Not to mention the fact that, now more than ever before, there is stakeholder pressure to ensure events deliver measurable returns—to quantify the effects of their events. Event planners now need to prove how successful their events have been, and to answer the question "What was the outcome of the event?"

So, who organizes corporate events?

Events increasingly form a key part of many an organization's marketing strategy. Why? Because events allow your audience to actually experience your company, its people and services before they buy. They can also look somebody in the eye and have a one-to-one dialogue about what matters to them. Corporate events are also a way of acquiring and or retaining customers. In these cases it is imperative that the event delivers audiences with a great company experience: something that inspires them to action—to call you, sign up and want to work with you. For these reasons events are immensely powerful. The issue for the event planner is, therefore, how you create a fabulous and lasting impression on the audience and so ensure they remember you for all the right reasons. Even for events involving only your staff, such as team building and away days, the principle of creating a great impression still holds true.

Events are therefore the ultimate live marketing experience. Get it right and great things can happen; get it wrong and your reputation can be damaged. Follow the advice in this book and you will get it right.

What types of organizations are currently delivering corporate events? Any of the following: businesses, local authorities, county councils, government departments, venues, visitor attractions, museums, charities, associations, galleries, hotels, universities, schools and, of course, individuals. Most people in fact!

The events they organize can include:

- Conferences
- Seminars
- Meetings
- Networking
- Dinners
- Staff parties
- Team building

- Away days
- Media or press launch
- Product launch or showcasing a new product or service
- Exhibitions
- Community project or fundraiser
- Brand awareness
- Employee appreciation
- Client reward or recognition
- Supplier appreciation
- Annual general meetings
- Milestones and anniversaries
- Open days and tours
- Awards and tributes
- Attracting new clients
- Opening or closing ceremonies
- Open days
- State, royal or VIP visits
- Ceremonial occasions and celebrations
- Careers and recruitment
- Naming ceremonies or topping out new buildings

Event management

On the face of it, planning an event may seem quite straightforward. Of course, like many things in life, something that seemed in essence quite simple may soon prove to be complicated. If you have already been involved in planning events, you will no doubt have discovered that they tend to become all-consuming, taxing your determination, your energy and your emotional reserves. This is because designing, planning and delivering events is a bit like directing a live stage show. However, unlike a show, there are usually no dress rehearsals or safety nets and, once your event has started, there are no second chances.

The good news is that I believe we can all be great event planners. So whether it is a meeting for 20 or a large conference for hundreds, my tried and tested 8-Step Event Planning Process will help you deliver a successful event.

Inside this book, you will learn the "how to" of:

- ✓ Delivering your event set against the principles of The Event Expert planning process
- ✓ Delivering an event your customers actually want
- ✓ Using objective setting to guide your event planning
- ✓ Creating and designing an event that excites: agreeing the look, style, format and positioning for the event, setting dates, evaluating and selecting the best ideas, theming your event, setting objectives and writing an event brief
- ✓ Event project planning: creating project plans, budgeting, picking your event team, selecting competent contractors, drafting event outlines, insurances, traffic management plans and contracts
- ✓ Selecting your venue criteria, searching and evaluating your venue, making site visits, getting venue quotes and preparing an event site plan
- ✓ Designing a great event programme: booking activities, speakers, entertainment and event catering, encouraging participation, setting event timings, delivering powerful presentations
- ✓ Creating compelling copy, using a variety of promotional media and calls to action, selling the benefits, using social media, pricing your event, incentivising attendance with bonuses, and defining methods of payment and registration
- ✓ Delivering your event: operational planning, managing your suppliers, contractor and speaker requirements, catering schedules, providing registration desks and

joining instructions, carrying out risk assessments and emergency planning
- ✓ Leading, motivating and briefing your event day team
- ✓ Obtaining feedback and evaluating the effect of your event

In short . . . how to deliver a successful and rewarding event that is packed full of great takeaway memories.

What this book will not do for you

This book will not give you the answers to specific questions about each different type of event. You will need to use your own in-depth knowledge of the subject matter to do that. Neither will it find you the perfect venue, give you details of the best event contractors or tell you which stage set, lighting gear or sound system is best for you.

Remember: this book is about event planning. The imaginative execution is down to you and your event team. However, this book will give you a great start, as will reading about and attending other events. It helps if you have an appetite for learning. You must also be willing (as I still am) to seek technical advice from relevant professionals from time to time.

As with anything in life, the more you practise events, the better and more confident you will become. With practice comes experience; with experience comes confidence. Real-life event experience will make you a better event manager because you have fought those event battles. You were there. Just remember, too, that event planning could be one of your untapped skills, something you did not know you were good at. So why not give it a go? The problem is, of course, that you will have to practise in public and you will make mistakes. I did and I survived!

Remember, events are "live" projects but, unlike most projects, they have a very definite and very public end date—event day!

My 8-Step Event Planning System

Although every event is different, well-planned events all share the same core principles, whatever their size or type. Because event management can seem a little chaotic at times, it will be your job to bring order to the proceedings and use strong leadership to keep everyone on track. My 8-Step Event Planning System will help you do this.

The 8-Step Event Planning System in brief:

1. **Purpose**—why run an event, who is the audience, why might they attend and what evidence is there to suggest it is a good idea?
2. **Presentation**—event design and creation, themes, date setting, idea evaluation, date setting, event briefs
3. **Planning**—project plans, project teams, budgeting, contractors, infrastructure, planning for safety, insurance, contracts
4. **Places**—choosing and evaluating your event venue, site planning
5. **Programme**—designing and delivering an engaging and interesting event programme
6. **Promotion**—creating effective event promotional plans and activities, ticketing, web sites
7. **Production**—making your festival happen, operational plans, risk assessments, event day teams, front-of-house operations
8. **People**—leading your event team, event evaluation

What makes a well-planned, memorable and effective event?

Just to get you thinking, let us take a look at the key ingredients of a great event:

- A definite purpose for the event—why are you running it, what are its aims?
- Clear and agreed objectives—what are you trying to achieve?
- Good organizational structure—do you have good reporting mechanisms and sufficient resources to do a good job?
- A committed team—everyone is committed to the event and its success
- A high-calibre leader—that is probably you!
- Precise and detailed planning—attention to detail is the key; everything is done properly or not at all
- Realistic timescales—do not take shortcuts; can you achieve everything you want to achieve in the time available?
- Efficient and effective communication—ensure everyone knows what is happening and when
- Contingency plans—what could go wrong and what is your plan for dealing with it?
- Effective publicity that is interesting and targeted—if you do not tell people about the event, they will not come
- The welcome—a warm friendly one is vital; a smile and first impressions count
- Excellent customer care—ensure everyone provides fantastic service throughout the whole event; if your staff are not good at this, the audience will not come back or recommend you to their colleagues and networks
- The event programme—speakers, artistes, attractions, entertainment, activities—should run on schedule and be varied in style and format

7

- Pricing structure—your audience can afford it and perceive it to be good value for money
- Food and refreshments—are they appropriate and adequate?
- The look and feel—create the right atmosphere
- Venues—ensure they are clean, comfortable, convenient, with professional staff and great internal event signage
- A great master of ceremonies—this person will bring your event to life
- The event itself—make sure is enjoyable, memorable; think "we've had a good time and spent our time with like-minded people"
- A thank you on departure in person—and perhaps with a bespoke gift or access to presentations

In the early stages of planning an event, it pays to be curious, ask many questions and really listen to the responses. One of the biggest reasons for asking questions is to avoid making assumptions. You cannot afford to assume understanding. You must confirm it. You also need to ask the sometimes tricky "Why?" question as you need to have a very clear picture in your head about what sort of event you are trying to deliver in order to achieve the best result. Remember: events will be important to you, your organization, your partners and your sponsors—in fact, to everyone involved in organizing and participating in them. It pays to make sure you have the time, energy and support to do the best job you can.

Top tip

If you do not ask, they cannot say "yes". Similarly, if you do not ask, the answer will always be "no".

CHAPTER 2

PURPOSE: CREATING EVENTS THAT AUDIENCES WANT TO ATTEND

Having a great event idea is one thing; finding a receptive and enthusiastic audience in sufficient numbers is another altogether. Developing the type of events that potential visitors would like to attend or participate in requires you to do a little research. Do remember that your event will become of genuine interest to people when you provide content and an experience that other organizations are not providing. You need to find out what they think, what they need right now and, just as importantly, what your competitors are doing.

Typically, you are looking for answers to the following:

1. Are there any emerging trends in your world or theirs?
2. Are there any new activities, products, services or working practices that are beginning to make waves or are doing well in other relevant sectors?
3. Have you already identified demand?
4. Is there a sizeable enough target market, namely a community of people, businesses or organizations to

sell to in order to make your event idea a viable and successful one? Who do you think your events' primary target markets are as well as any secondary or tertiary markets?

5. You must also ascertain what kinds of events your competitors already run. Are they in the same geographical area and/or the same business category as you? Now ask yourself, "Can I or should I compete with them in terms of appeal or available budget?"

At this point, it is also wise to carry out a SWOT analysis. It will help you understand the internal and external operating environment for your event proposal by examining its strengths, weaknesses, opportunities and threats.

Event SWOT analysis

Internal environment

Strengths—these can include the level of expertise, quality of suppliers, access or ownership of the venue, financial resources, facilities and equipment, available financial resources and links to potential sponsors

Weaknesses—the opposite of the items listed as strengths, such as no relevant expertise

External environment

Opportunities—these can include current favourable conditions, the current economic situation, social and cultural factors, changes in the way we do business, technological factors, demographics (enough of the right people), concerns about the environment, competition from other events, the introduction of new innovations or products (whether you can get in first)

Threats—the opposite of the items listed as opportunities, such as unfavourable economic, social, business or political conditions

Conducting this kind of research is a useful exercise, so you can find out where you are, plug any gaps in knowledge, understand what you are up against and take advantage of any developments or trends that will help your cause. You need to have a good understanding of the market you operate in. If you have a marketing team, their work should help guide your event design. You can, of course, find out a lot of information by reading your industry press, following the key influencers in your world and searching the internet.

Why are you running this event?

Each event should have one main overarching purpose but can have a couple of subsidiary objectives, too. For example:

1. The main purpose of a press or product launch would be to achieve X amount of column inches or media coverage in all relevant industry media
2. You may attend a careers or job fair with the intention of finding 20 new graduate candidates
3. You may take a stand at an industry exhibition with the intention of collecting 100 potential leads
4. You may arrange an away day for senior managers with the intention of planning next year's activities; the purpose of the day is to produce the plan

Your audience could be at your event for a variety of reasons, too, such as to network, sell, buy and learn.

I have listed below the types of reasons why businesses run events. Work your way through the list and consider the reasons why you are running your next event:

- Exchange information or ideas
- Provide training
- Educate, enlighten, expose people to new ideas or ways of thinking
- Thank suppliers, clients, partners
- Awards, anniversaries, celebration
- Support a company-sponsored charity or project
- For a partner organization
- Celebrate milestones, national occasions, campaigns
- Develop a mailing list
- For competition
- For fun, entertainment, excitement, escapism, nostalgia
- Raise money for a good cause
- Send a message
- Increase brand awareness
- Improve quality of life, feel-good factor, to make a difference
- Recruit or retain new or existing people

You now need to select one overarching event aim, which is the reason why you want to run an event, and choose subsidiary aims if you need to. Everyone on your event planning team should agree to your aims.

Knowing "why" makes your life a lot easier. It gives direction to your event planning and ensures that you channel all your energies into achieving your overarching aim. It also helps you to say "yes" to ideas and activities that support the cause and "no thank you" to those who do not.

Who are you running this event for?

Without putting too fine a point on it, events need audiences or they fail. You therefore need to have a clear idea as to who your likely attendees will be. In other words, who is likely to want to come to or benefit from your event? Consider whether they are:

- Your signed-up supporters, previous clients or newsletter readers
- A new untapped market
- The business community as a whole
- A particular sector of the business community
- A particular type of attendee
- A sector of your local population in terms of age, gender, location or interest
- A predetermined audience, such as invited guests or dignitaries

If you cannot describe your audience, who they are and where to find them, how can you possibly provide them with an event they want? You need to create a customer profile. You want to understand where they "hang out" (business or social), what they are talking about and what their concerns are right now. You will need to agree what size of company you want to target, what their sector is and where they are located. Ascertaining information about the types of roles potential audience members will perform and at what level is also vital.

Having decided on your audience, work out how far they are likely to travel to an event and whether they have any known time constraints, such as times of the day or year that will not suit them. Ultimately, you need to be confident that you will have enough of the right people with the right mind set (bearing in mind most may not want to attend) to make your idea a financially viable one.

What do others think about your event idea?

Armed with a very basic outline of what you think your event could be, it is time to establish what other people think of your idea. If you are anticipating spending a large amount of your organization's money, they will want to see some evidence that this is not just a spur-of-the-moment idea but is going to be money and time well spent. Talk to your colleagues and anybody else you might know whose opinion you value. You might be amazed at what they come back with: observations, advice, contacts and even (if you are really lucky) offers of help.

It is also important to find out what your target audience thinks of your idea. You could conduct a short survey with a few questions about your event plans. Do you have a list of clients, a list of newsletter subscribers or information about previous event attendees? If so, select a sample and send them a short survey as follows:

- We [organization] are thinking of organizing [type of event] because we want to [reason for the event]
- It will be at the [XYZ] venue
- It will be at [24-hour time] on [date]
- The event programme will include [give outline details of the event programme, for example workshops, speeches, entertainment, ticket price]
- Please tell us what you think about this
- Would you consider attending this event?

There are a number of online survey tools you could use. However, I do think such surveys have more impact if they come directly from the company asking for the information. You will also get more meaningful responses from your own lists. You may have to offer an incentive to complete the survey. You will not get a reply from everyone, but any sort of feedback will be useful.

By the way, at this stage, it is also wise to make a list of potential partners, organizations or people who might also be interested in helping or working with you. Would you consider a joint venture and double your marketing reach. Arrange to speak to them about the general purpose, type of event, likely date and venue and find out what they think. If there is genuine enthusiasm for your event, and other organizations like what you are proposing, you can now start to think about how to design an event to achieve your agreed purpose.

In summary

- Do your research. Identify a need, target group(s), an emerging trend and the competition. Consider who you are likely to be competing with.
- Gather some evidence. Is it a good idea? Is there enough interest to give you a reasonable chance of providing an event that people actually want?
- For certain types of corporate events, you need to be sure that your planned event is going to provide the content, the insights and the new ways of working that your audience actually wants. If your intended audience can find out your information somewhere else, they might just go somewhere else instead.
- Do your homework. You need to learn who your target audience is and then create a customer profile.
- As a basic minimum, all events need a clear statement of purpose, a vision that should underpin all your event planning activities.
- Remember that going to an event must, as a basic minimum, feel like a valuable and worthwhile use of somebody's time. Conducting research will help you to create worthwhile event experiences.

CHAPTER 3

PRESENTATION: DESIGNING MUST-ATTEND EVENTS

With a clear idea of why and who you are planning your event for, and an indication that others think your idea is a good one, you are now ready to start designing the event. It is now time to consider what your event is going to look and feel like. What are people going to do, learn and take part in? Does it need a theme? And, crucially, what sort of takeaway memories do you want your visitors to leave your event with? "I loved it." "I like the way your organization does things." "I have learnt something." "I think I'd like to work with you, so please keep in touch." And, of course, you'd like them to say: "What a great event."

At the presentation stage, what you are trying to do is create a blueprint of your proposed event in words, pictures, images and numbers but always with your agreed objectives at the forefront of your thinking. At this stage, you want to be thinking about the journey that a delegate or guest is going to take, from the moment they arrive at your event to the moment they leave. What will their event experience actually be like?

If you usually take on everything yourself, now might be a good time to recognize that designing a great event is not something you can easily do on your own. To help you generate lots of ideas, look for people who have creative flair and a range of different experiences and interests to help you. Between five and eight people is an ideal number for ensuring a great event brainstorming session.

Running an event brainstorming meeting

For these meetings to be both effective and creative, try to remove all thoughts of actual and perceived boundaries (including budgets) and allow attendees to let their imaginations run wild. Before you start being all-creative, you need to agree what type of event it is going to be. The options are generally as follows:

- Indoor, outdoor, under canvas
- Evening, afternoon, day, weekend, week-long
- Free, paid, combination
- Local, regional, national, international in scale or appeal
- Special, one-off, celebration of a moment in time, company milestone, new campaign, new product

At the start of the meeting, tell your colleagues your reason for organizing the event and for whom you are organizing it. The following list will help you focus the meeting's creative thoughts:

- Creating an event theme (more about themes later)
- Different formats of games, competitions, create your company game
- Can you use music during the event, live or recorded?
- Bespoke structures, stages, marquees

- Interesting venues
- Projection systems and plasma screens to improve delegate experience
- Tours and visits
- Speakers, presentations, workshops
- Things to do, take part in, play and learn
- A varied programme of activities: games, quizzes, mass participatory activities, acts, videos, demonstrations
- Decoration, tables, venue, room
- Food to eat, to make, to learn about
- Dress, uniforms, costumes
- Sights, sounds, smells
- Lighting effects to add atmosphere
- Would different modes of transport enhance your event?
- Gifts, giveaways
- Art in its many different forms
- The five senses: touch (textures), smell (scented candles), taste (catering), sight (colours) and hearing (music); can you incorporate them all?
- Sensible and relevant "wow" factors

As the meeting chair, your role is to encourage participation and not to pass comment or judgement on any of the ideas. You will need to make a note of every idea or suggestion. You must also ensure that everyone feels comfortable enough to suggest any of their ideas, however wacky they may seem to you and or other team members.

Be aware of these traditional creativity killers

"The old ideas or ways of doing things are very tempting—they are safe, often-cherished notions."

You just cannot let go of the past. However, you must try!

"Why change? We have looked at last year's feedback and see no reason to make changes. The delegates in the main say nice things about our events."

You need to ask whether enough of your audience really say these things, or if they are just being polite. Maintaining the status quo will precipitate the beginning of the end for your events, sooner than you think.

"This is how the corporate events world does events, so we'd best do the same."

This is a problem with rigidity, in thinking you need to conform. In my opinion, many of the corporate events I attend do all look and feel the same. This is not the way to stand out from the competition.

Here is a nice quote about opening up your mind to the possibilities:

"Beyond areas of right and wrong there is a field. I will meet you there." (Russi)

Using an event theme

While some of your events, because of their subject matter, already have a theme, the way in which you present it can take many forms. Your event theming can be very elaborate, involving a wide range of different elements, or it can be a much simpler affair.

Think of the unusual. Clever themes can be used to spark discussion amongst your guests and can leave a lasting impression. Once agreed, all elements of the event must then fit the theme in a relevant and consistent way, with perhaps the odd "wow", too. Anything can be used as an event theme: colours, numbers, historical events, exercise, fashions, statements, campaigns, legislation, films, countries, games and so forth. So, what aspects of your event can be themed?

- The venue—inside and outside
- Infrastructure—marquees, staging, barriers
- Catering—food, drinks, table settings, serving staff
- Audiovisual—sound, lighting
- Special effects—lasers, fireworks
- Speakers, entertainment, artistes
- Decoration, props, scenery, flowers, colours (colours can affect the mood)
- Sounds, music
- All forms of communication—invitations, web sites, posters,
- Transport
- Dress code
- Gifts and favours
- Event staff—male, female, uniform, look, style

How much you let the theme dictate your event design will ultimately be a factor of how much money you have to spend and how creative you are in finding alternative solutions to some of the more costly theming elements. There are a number of companies that specialize in theming events. If you have the budget, a call to them may be a good idea.

Selecting the best idea

Having made a note of all the ideas generated at your creative brainstorming meeting, it is now time to start sifting through them and reducing this long list of ideas into a shorter list that the team really likes. You could perhaps include a couple of "wild card" ideas, or things you would not normally consider. Your list will include ideas that are incomplete but considered to be of sufficient interest to warrant further work. With your ideas to hand, it is now necessary to make a more reasoned assessment of the relative merits of each idea.

I suggest you evaluate your thoughts against the following five criteria.

1. How well does your idea match up with your original event purpose and your reason for organising the event in the first place?
2. Consider audience acceptance (marketing). Try testing your ideas out on a few people who you think might attend and see what they say. Do they like it? Do they understand what they are coming to? Would they recommend it to a friend?
3. Can you afford it (financially)? You now need to start getting some estimates in place to give you some idea of how much your event is going to cost, what the opportunity cost is and (if relevant) how much money it might raise.
4. Can you or your team plan and deliver the event successfully (operationally)? Do you have the skills to organize the event? Do you need to buy in or recruit some expert help, or both?
5. This section is for the "well, I just like it" type of ideas. These ideas just capture your imagination and, while they possibly do not meet all the assessment criteria above, they "feel" right. You should only include one or two of these types of ideas in your event. They can be used as a way of testing the water.

Having now completed your evaluation, you will have all the information you need to decide exactly what type and style of event you are going to organize.

Setting an event date

Setting your event date is an important decision. Your primary concern is always making sure that you set a date and time to suit your target audience. The following list of factors will help you set your event date:

- Target the general availability of your audience
- Known audience time limiters, such as working hours and ethos
- Past event history
- Likely weather conditions at the time of year, especially if the event is dependent on location or time of year
- Other local corporate events
- School holidays
- National events, such as key sporting, political, annual and one-off national occasions
- Availability of key services, activities and people
- Competing with long weekends over a bank holiday, when many people go on holiday or take an extra day of leave
- Significant religious occasions
- Other events at the same venue, restricting options such as parking or catering
- Availability of the venue
- International working practices
- Accepted norms, such as busy times of the year, for your audience

Before setting your event date, please ensure you really do your research to establish just what is the best time and day for your audience. Do not assume you know.

Setting some event objectives

You will now have a good idea about what you want to do. To ensure your event can demonstrate real value for money or effort, it is worth setting some objectives. These will give your event team something to aim for and something against which to measure the success of the event. Coming up with a return-on-event figure for events is not always easy, as in some cases it may be more about the experience, but you do need some sort of target to aim for. Here are some examples:

- Number of attendees
- Numbers signed up
- Requests for further information
- Requests for further meetings
- Units sold
- Raised awareness (more people now know about your products and services)
- Awards achieved

The general rule of thumb on objective setting is to make your objectives:

- Specific
- Measurable
- Achievable
- Realistic
- Timed
- Challenging

In order to get a true measure of the success of your event, and whether it has fulfilled its objectives, you will need to know all your costs and sources of income. More about this in Chapter 8.

Writing an event brief

You now have all the information you need to write a complete description of the task: an event brief. Some of you may, in fact, have been given a brief from your team, a line manager, a corporate director or your partner agency. Wherever it has come from, your event brief should cover the following:

- Background information about the organization
- Target audience—what sort of people you want to attract and a guesstimate of how many people you think will attend
- Principal purpose, outcome
- Timelines, dates
- Outline of the programme, such as demonstrations, speakers, workshops
- Any "must happens", such as a speech, awards
- The budget

Writing an event proposal report

To justify the time and resources you have spent on your event so far, or for funding purposes, you are likely to have to write a report that addresses the following subject areas:

- Concept and vision
- Desired objectives
- How the event will fulfil the objectives
- Evidence of demand, past or current, or both
- Your experience, track record, expertise
- How it will be achievable and appropriate
- Costs versus projected income, acceptable risk
- Attractiveness to sponsors (please be honest) or grant-making bodies, or both

- How it will be inclusive, spectacular, distinctive and popular
- Established interest from partners and stakeholders
- Ability to attract a new audience or develop an existing audience
- Venue, time and day
- How it will appeal to audiences (local, regional, national or international)

Deciding what to call your event

There are no hard and fast rules here but getting the right name is important. Catchy, memorable, relevant and not too clever generally works. The obvious works well, too: it is what it says on the poster. Make sure it is clear and concise, and that everybody understands what it is. So how do you find the perfect event name? The following may help:

- Brainstorm some ideas
- Do searches—somebody else may already be using your event name and, as most of us use search engines to find information, you need them to find your event easily; list your search results
- Test the market—find out what other people think of it and, importantly, if they "get it" or understand what it is without having to call you up on the phone! (It could be worth seeking advice from graphic designers, too.)
- Decide whether your event name needs a strapline, something that encapsulates what your event is in just a few words—the strapline needs to talk to your audience, so consider what might be their most likely reason for attending your event
- Finally, get everyone's agreement for the event name and strapline—then you get to the exciting stage of seeing what it could look light in print!

In summary

- The design stage can be a lot of fun and you have to be able to open your mind up to the possibilities and be brave; try something different.
- At this part of the process, remember that "creative thinking without boundaries" always works best. It is the time to ignore the restraints of practicality, cost, scale or viability; it is the time to dream, so no idea is a bad idea.
- The objective of the brainstorming sessions is to try to uncover an idea that resonates with and inspires everyone.
- Try to be consumer-led and inspired. Will your event provide the solution(s) to your customer's problems? Will your target audience value it?
- Consider what your event's "game changer" might be. What is the audience going to hear for the first time that will make a difference to them? Too many events are too predictable. We often know who is going to say what at an event before we get there, so all we need is a copy of the event's notes to read later.
- It is wise to remember that the more an event is perceived by its audience to have emerged from within its ranks (if, for example, they have asked for it), the greater is the likelihood that your event will be successful. In other words, we own what we help to create.
- The best event designers are always willing to attend a wide variety of other organizations' events. They also like to read about events and to spend time researching ideas and reviewing the events press. This is where they get their event ideas.
- Always set yourself some event objectives, something to aim for.
- There are very few instant successes in the corporate events world. Events take time to build an audience

and a reputation. Some of your events will fail. Failure is always a possibility but, when the "corporates" indicate that failure is not an option, you might find that your team's creativity is severely challenged. Your team becomes scared of failure and reverts to what is "safe", thinking that "it worked in the past, so it might work again". You just need to persevere.

CHAPTER 4

PLANNING: EASY STEPS TO SUCCESSFUL EVENTS

Now you have a clear idea of the what, who, why, where and when of your event (your event brief), it's time to start planning it—to make it happen.

Much of the success of your event will be down to just how much time and effort you put into planning it. Every element of your event will require discussion and decisions. At the event planning stage, it is all about the detail, your ability to drive the process forward, stick to the agreed event aim and hit those key deadlines.

This stage is primarily concerned with the result, the means of achieving it and delivering that all-important high-quality event experience. It is in the planning stage that you put together your event team, prepare the project plan, search for and hire competent contractors, brief a production company, establish what insurance your event needs, agree contracts and start planning for a safe event.

Recruiting your event planning team

An event planning team usually consists of two to ten people and comprises your immediate colleagues, departmental representatives, committee members, partner organizations and any outside experts you need to fill any gaps in understanding or skills. Many, if not all, of your team members may be volunteering in addition to their normal job, so make sure all meetings run to time and agenda.

You must hold and schedule regular event planning meetings, which should be purposeful and productive occasions designed to solve problems, stimulate ideas and generate action. Each meeting must have an agenda, minutes, action points, and a start and finish time. Typical agenda items are as follows:

- Introductions and welcomes
- Apologies
- Minutes of last meeting
- Review of event project plan
- Event programme review and update
- Budget review and update
- Venue search, evaluation and site planning
- Exhibitors update
- Staff review and update
- Marketing plan review and update
- Agree priority work areas
- Event day operational planning
- Set next project team meeting
- Any other business

These meetings will play a crucial role in ensuring the success of your event. Each team member should be assigned roles and responsibilities and everyone will need to understand that it is critical that they pull their weight. Ultimately, the success of your event will depend on the quality of your team, how well they work together and your ability to lead them.

Event project plans

A Gantt chart (which is a type of bar chart, with the "bars" running horizontally) created in Microsoft Excel generally works in terms of managing the planning process for the event. It also provides you and your team with a visual representation of your event. There is also a range of project management software on the market if you prefer this type of option.

Like any other project, there will be a series of sequential (and parallel) tasks with deadlines. You can establish these by looking at the key areas listed below, creating tasks and setting start and end dates as well as key milestones. The meeting of these key milestones could be critical to the overall success of the event.

Typically, your event project plan will include tasks relating to the following key work areas:

- Setting of event aims and objectives
- Design and creative tasks—brainstorming, themes, event briefs
- Venues—selection, site visit, booking, site planning
- Planning—infrastructure requirements, contractors, insurance, health and safety, risk assessments, event management plans
- Programming—timings, booking of key personnel, joining instructions
- Operational tasks—relating to the set-up, running and breakdown (clearing away or dismantling) of the event, and the event day teams, arrivals and departures

- Finance—securing funding, costing, budgeting, sponsorship
- Marketing—pricing, all promotional activities, public relations
- Administration—updating and project plan review, sending out information, signing contracts

A word of warning: each one of these work areas will need to appear in the event project plan on more than one occasion. They are not actions completed in one go. You will have to revisit them on several occasions. For an event project plan to be of real assistance, it needs to contain a comprehensive set of actions and realistic timescales and to be driven forward by an event planner who injects "continuous urgency" into the process, making sure things get done. Creating event project plans are not, however, one-off exercises. They are active documents that require regular review and adaptation to changing circumstances.

Top tip

What an event project plan will not do for you is make something happen. You must do that. Keep driving your event forward and never let it stall.

Recruiting your event day team members, their roles and organizational structure

Your *event planning* team will always be smaller in number than your *event day* team. You will need to recruit more people to help you actually deliver the event. Ensuring your events are adequately staffed with the right people, who are appropriately trained, motivated and organized, is something that all event planners must do. Getting the right event staff will take time, but the sooner you start thinking about whom you need, the more likely you are to get the people you want.

You will need to:

- Identify all tasks associated with delivering your event
- Determine how many staff, volunteers and team leaders you will need
- Determine if they need any specialist skills, experience or qualifications
- Create a very brief job description and person specification
- Seek to recruit or persuade, then interview, select, contract, and induct or train them
- Create a "family tree"—listing "who does what" is useful at this stage

For most of us, this process can be completed with a quick chat and writing a few basic briefing notes. Please do not forget any necessary legal employment requirements, if appropriate. This process will, of course, be simpler if you are working with your own colleagues. However, you should still be trying to match tasks to talents. The types of people or roles you may require on event day are as follows:

- Event day car parkers, traffic marshals
- Welcome, reception, registration
- Ticket office sellers, supervisors, programme sellers, food servers
- Ticket or pass checkers, ushers
- Security (inside and outside, and ideally security industry-trained)
- Information area or stand
- Event stewards, site or floor walking
- Events set-up and breakdown crew

- Clean-up crew, litter pickers (before, during and after the event)
- Event managers
- Programme managers to run the programme
- Runners
- First aiders (private medical providers, NHS, Red Cross, St John Ambulance)
- Catering staff
- Press officers
- Exhibitor or stallholder manager

You are not necessarily looking to fill every one of these roles with an individual(s), as many of these roles can be fulfilled by the same person or a small team of the right kind of people.

You event day team is likely to be a mix of professionally qualified staff and volunteers. However, your team on occasions can be made up entirely of volunteers. This will depend on the event.

And in addition to your own event day team, you will be adding specialist personnel such as caterers, electricians and audio-visual staff.

What will you expect your event day team to do?

Your event day team should:

- Know who's who on site
- Control traffic movements on site, in and out of the car parks
- Carry out fire and no smoking patrols
- Keep emergency routes and gangways clear at all times
- Deal with enquiries and logging accidents
- Give advice on the event programme

- Learn the site layout and the location of key facilities, entrances, exits and first aid points
- Keep an eye out for any overcrowding issues, particularly near entrances and exits
- Monitor the audience, guests and crowds
- Be aware of the location and be able to use fire-fighting equipment
- Know what to do in an emergency
- Keep the site clear of litter
- Concentrate on their duties and only leave their post when told to do so
- Wear clothing that clearly identifies them as event personnel
- Remain calm and courteous towards visitors and members of the public at all times

Above all else, look for people with a genuine passion for events, those who enjoy the live and somewhat pressured environment of event production and who have a "can do" attitude. The right "on the day" event team will ensure that your audience will have a safer, more relaxed and enjoyable time at your event.

It is a good idea to create a briefing pack for all staff. In most cases, this can be a couple of sheets of A4 outlining all the key event information they need to know. It is also helpful to include a list of the main players' mobile phone numbers. I would strongly recommend that the event manager also hold a full staff briefing prior to doors opening, to remind everybody of their duties and to answer any last-minute questions. I will talk about your event day team in more detail in Chapter 8.

Picking the right contractors

You may need to hire outside contractors to provide you with services such as:

- Portable toilets units—from single units to fully plumbed trailers
- Marquees—of all shapes and sizes
- Stages—of any size for indoor use or covered for outdoor use
- Fencing or barriers to guide people or keep them out
- Event communications (for staff)—two-way radios
- Event communications (for the audience)—public address systems
- Facilities for people with disabilities—ramps, viewing areas, specialist toilets
- Electrical contractor—providing cabling, lighting, connection to power source
- AA or RAC traffic directional signs
- Catering—outside units, mobile caterer, hire of kitchen units
- Waste disposal—bins, litter pickers
- Fire prevention systems—fire extinguishers, fire blankets, sand buckets, no smoking signs
- Audiovisual—laptop, screen, lectern, microphone, flipchart, use of Wi-Fi/internet connection, use of video and sound
- Lighting—indoors and outdoors
- Sound systems—from very small to very large, public address systems
- Power—small to large generators
- Fireworks, special effects, lasers
- Decoration—flowers, balloons, props, table centres
- Transport companies—taxis, coaches, buses
- Cleaning—venue, toilets
- Stewards, staff, security—times, numbers, roles

- First aid—St John Ambulance, Red Cross, NHS
- Video, television, live streaming, outside broadcast

You can find these contractors in the normal way through search engines, Yellow Pages, Thompson Local and sector-specific trade associations. However, if you know of colleagues who have put on events before, they may be able to suggest reliable contractors. You then need to ask them the following to establish their competence and experience:

- Has the company written a risk assessment for the services they provide and have they implemented any necessary control measures?
- Do they have a current health and safety policy?

You should also ask them to provide:

- The name, company, addresses and telephone numbers of two references
- A copy of the company Public Liability Insurance Certificate
- A copy of the company Employers' Liability Insurance Policy
- A copy of the company Product Liability Insurance Policy
- A copy of their risk assessment that specifically covers the services being provided to your event; please ensure you do not accept a generic company risk assessment
- A copy of their Professional Indemnity Insurance Policy

Whilst you might think this is a little over the top, consider the consequential loss of money and reputation if you do not undertake some basic checks and then there is an accident. You must find, and only work with, *competent* contractors. They will have all of the above paperwork to hand.

Contracts

It is imperative you have a signed contract with all of your key service providers. It will give both parties the reassurance that comes from knowing exactly what they have agreed to and what happens if you or they break the agreement in any way. Event organizers must know where their legal responsibilities start and end.

As a basic minimum, your contract will have the following headings:

- The parties
- Definitions of services
- General conditions and rights
- Term (with dates)
- Price
- Payment
- Delivery conditions
- Obligations of both parties, warranties, liabilities, insurance
- Assignment or sub-contracting
- Force majeure (such as acts of God, fire and flood)
- Termination rights, breach, and insolvency (and consider what would count as a breach)
- Disputes and jurisdiction
- Signatures

Something else to make sure you understand is what you would be liable for, and when, if things were to go wrong. Are they indicating the cancellation period in days or working days? There is an important difference. Acts and speakers can still require payment even if they do not turn up. Be wary; read the contract.

You should have a contract in place for the following, if you are using them:

- Venue hire
- Speakers, entertainers
- Ticket agency
- Event management company
- Suppliers
- Caterers
- Event staff (possibly through an agency)

Planning for a safe event

Different factors may affect the safety and security of your attendees. The following list is by no means exhaustive, but will give you some idea about where to focus your attention.

Venue

Know your venue's permitted uses. Does it have an appropriate management system set up for these types of events? Is it a suitable venue for the event? What is its occupant capacity? What safety checks do they carry out?

Event manager

You must have a designated, named individual as the event manager (which is necessary for a licence application). You also need competent staff who are trained or expert.

Audience management

How do you intend to manage your audience? What type of stewards or security will you need? What is the profile of your audience (age, male, female, numbers)? You will also need to consider how you manage entrance and activity queues and know how many people are on site. You must also have a system in place to communicate with your stewards.

Communications

How will you communicate with staff? Mobiles, two-way radios? Staff need to be informed who their points of contact are, for example in case of an emergency. How will you communicate with the audience? A public address system or a loudhailer.

Means of escape

You will need to provide clear signage directing people to the emergency exits (essential for indoor or enclosed outdoor venues), keep gangways and exits clear of obstructions, create safe places (fire assembly points) and mark all exits on the site plan.

Fire precautions

You must have portable fire-fighting equipment on the site, and staff should be trained to use it. You must keep your event site clear of rubbish or possible sources of ignition. Certain items must also carry fire retardancy properties too (they have a greater resistance to fire, allowing you more time to evacuate your event space). If you are hiring the venue, the onus is on the venue to have all this is place. You and your team just need to know what to do in the case of a fire.

Lighting and heating

These need to be adequate for normal use. All electrical systems associated with lighting and heating must have a system in place to prevent unauthorized access. At certain times of the year and for outdoor events or events in a marquee, you may also need to provide temporary lighting towers and heating systems.

Electrical installations

You will need to agree how you can access any local power supplies for normal operational use. Again, for outdoor events, you may also need to provide portable electrical generators. These will need securing (fencing off) and earthing. All electrical wiring must be covered, flown or buried and installed by a qualified electrician who will test and inspect the work.

Structures

You may need to consider using temporary structures, such as marquees and stages. You will therefore need to decide what purpose they will perform and what size they will need to be. They need to be *competently* installed, meet any appropriate structural regulations, be suitably located and carry safety certificates.

Barriers

Think about whether you require any form of fencing, where you need it and what purpose it needs to serve. Is it to guide people, for which you need ropes or poles for example, or to keep people out? In other words, is it fit for purpose?

Toilets

Consider the numbers of male and female toilets and urinals you need on site or at the venue. Do go and have a look at them and see if they are of suitable quality and in sufficient numbers to cope with peak usage (for example, during session breaks).

Establish from the venue what the cleaning regime will be during your event. This is important because you want to make sure the toilets remain clean and tidy throughout your event and not just at the start.

If you are using temporary toilet units, you will need to consider the availability of fresh water for topping up service tanks and hand-washing facilities. Similarly, you must have a toilet-cleaning regime in place too. The recommended ratios are as follows, but they are also dependent on exactly what type of event you are planning, so expect to vary these figures if required:

Events lasting over 6 hours	Events lasting less than 6 hours
Female	**Female**
1 toilet per 100 females	1 toilet per 120 females
Males	**Males**
1 toilet per 500 males, plus 1 urinal per 150 males	1 toilet per 600 males, plus 1 urinal per 175 males

Entertainment, performers, demonstrators, speakers

Consider the size and style of any performance arena you require. Will it need any technical requirements? If so, what? Will you need to provide barriers and or stewards or security in front of or around the stage area?

First aid

The type of event you organize along with the numbers of delegates you anticipate or know will turn out will dictate what number and type of first aid personnel you require. Again, if hiring a venue, the venue would be supplying this service and to the required level. It is wise to check to make sure there are no misunderstandings. You will need to know what to do and who to contact in the case of a medical emergency at your event. For outdoor events, you may have to arrange and pay for all first aid provision.

Seating arrangements

You must ensure that you and your event team keep all walkways, entrances and exits clear, inside and outside.

Staff

You will need to ensure that you hire or persuade only competent and trained individuals, organized into teams, in the right number and with clear roles and responsibilities. You should also hold a full staff briefing meeting and create an event day briefing pack.

Disability Discrimination Act (DDA)

Nowadays, all venues should be DDA compliant. It is good practice to ensure that you: remove any obstacles from your event site; provide clear information, viewing areas and disabled toilets; and repair any uneven surfaces or potential trip hazards.

Catering and refreshments

In terms of event safety, you will need to decide who will do your catering (for example, the venue or another catering company) and ensure that they have all the necessary food hygiene certificates, local authority registration details, insurance documentation and risk assessments. I will touch on this subject in more detail in Chapters 5 and 7.

Transport and traffic plan

For large events, it pays to consider the impact that the traffic to and from your event will have on the local area and transport systems. You will need to consider whether the venue has sufficient car parking facilities (at the time you want them). You should also provide good event day signing and traffic marshalling when your delegates arrive on site.

Insurance

Do ensure everyone providing services to or trading at your event carries valid insurance certificates, copies of which they sent to you prior to the event. Please do also check that your company insurances allow you to run events off campus.

Emergency plan

What will you do in the case of emergency? What is the venue's or your own evacuation procedure? What will your steward's duties be in an emergency and where are your places of safety and escape routes? You will need to be briefed by the venue and, if you are outdoors or under canvas, you will have to create your own emergency evacuation policy. You will find advice on emergency planning in Chapter 8.

Information point

It is always wise to provide a meeting or information point, or both, staffed with trained personnel.

Litter

You will need to provide staff to litter-pick throughout your event and empty rubbish bins as required. Either you do it yourself or you agree with the venue that they will do it.

Generally, the venue will provide this service but you do need to ask them and determine whether there will be an extra cost.

Security

You may need security. The type, roles and number of security you need will depend on your event and the audience. If you hire professional security people, they must be Security Industry Association (SIA) checked, badged and insured and they should carry an ID badge with a bar code and photo. Reputable security providers will help you decide what you need. If you are hiring a venue, many of these issues should be addressed to the venue manager.

The venue is responsible for the provision of a safe space that meets all the current building regulations. Please do not forget that you: the event manager is solely responsible for all other aspects of your event, its guests, contractors and all associated staff and activities.

Transport, traffic and parking plans

Even for relatively small events, it pays to consider how you intend to deal with the extra traffic and parking requirements created by your event attendees.

- Consider your event location, including where it is in relation to the surrounding road network, public transport, any park-and-ride schemes, car parks (the venues and any nearby additional car parks) and pedestrian access routes. Will the existing parking provision be enough? Find out the capacities and operating hours of the existing car parks. Are they enough to accommodate your estimate of the numbers of cars and coaches attending? Do not forget staff parking! If you do not have sufficient on-site parking, what are your nearby parking options?

- Will you need space to park coaches? If so, how many? Where do you want them to arrive, and where would be a suitable drop-off and pick-up point?
- Is your event venue already well signed and easy to find? If not, can you create some temporary event signing? Or can you afford to contract the AA Event Signing section. They will draw up a signing schedule, send you a quote and then request permission from the local authority or Highways Agency? Do you have, or can you create, emergency vehicle access routes into and around your site, if required?
- What arrangements do you have in place for disabled visitors wishing to park close to your event?

It is always wise to consider that visitors or participants tend to want to get to a venue using their typical mode of transport. Changing people's travelling habits is very hard to do, but we must try if your event venue is not suited to receiving a large number of cars. Consider whether the venue can be reached by public transport. Having a well-thought-out transport plan will play a key part in ensuring that your event runs smoothly, from start to finish. In other words, everybody arrives on time and at the right place and parks in the right places.

Event budgets

The event budget articulates your event's plans in monetary terms, so you should be able to look at it and get a good idea about how the event is being delivered. The budget has to be determined with the aims and objectives in mind. A big bold objective will require a big budget.

Event budgets are initially a mixture of fact and educated guess work. The budgetary process does impose some necessary financial discipline into the event planning process. The figures matter. There will be fixed costs, which stay the same whatever the size of the event, and variable costs, which go up or down according to attendance level. In my experience, many contractors do now accept that there may need to be an element of negotiation, so consider what you think is a good and fair deal.

It is always a good idea to build a 5% contingency figure into your budget to cover any unforeseen or additional costs. All items of expenditure must be supported by a formal quote, so ensuring a little more fact than guesswork!

The good news is that not everything has to cost money. Events can offer a range of opportunities for "in kind" deals where no money changes hand. For example, goods and services might be provided in exchange for promotional opportunities.

A few words of advice: once you have acquired all your quotes, it is better to defer the event if there is any sense that you are not going to get sufficient funding to deliver it in the high-quality way you intended.

At the outset, you will need to decide what your event financial strategy will be. By that, I mean consider whether you are seeking to:

- Break even, where income matches expenditure
- Make a profit and, if so, how much
- Spend the allocated budget
- Accept that you may make a loss of up to [X]%

Determining your event's break-even point is not just advisable, it is good practice too. The event manager must also keep control of the budget through regular reviews and discussions with the event's team. The budget needs to be a regular agenda item. Together, you will need to keep an eye on individual areas within the event as well as the overall event figure.

It is very easy to spend a lot of money on an event. It is a little harder, but necessary, to determine the value that each item of expenditure will bring to the event. This goes back to where you want to position your event in your audience's minds. Creating a great-looking event will always come at a price.

Securing event sponsorship

While it would always be nice to have all the money you need to run your event, you may need to seek sponsorship. Traditionally, events have been quite successful at attracting sponsors. In recent years, though, it has become a lot harder.

Many companies like to sponsor events because they value being in front of that audience. Events offer them unique social occasions to be with people who are often having a good time and who are more likely to accept well-considered marketing campaigns. While companies often like events, finding a willing sponsor and then matching them to the right event is not easy.

Sponsorship is not a donation or grant; it is a commercial deal between two or more parties. Certain characteristics typify a sponsorship deal, and event organizers need to be acutely aware of them. These characteristics include:

- An exchange of meaningful benefits
- Agreement between both parties that the exchange is worthwhile

- A likelihood that there will be changes from the original proposal
- A formal contract providing that both parties must deliver their share of the deal

The bottom line is that sponsors want impact, awareness and sales. They want results. It is a strategic marketing investment.

The sponsorship process will be as follows:

- The event organizer realises there is a funding shortfall
- The event organizer identifies potential event benefits
- There is agreement that there are, in fact, sufficient benefits to offer a sponsor
- There is broad organizational approval to seek commercial sponsorship
- Inappropriate sponsors are identified
- The benefits package is priced (the offer)
- Companies that might be interested are found, contacted and shortlisted
- The offer is pitched (the sponsorship package)
- Companies screen the offer (yes, no, request further information)
- The proposal is negotiated and a contract is sought
- The event organizer delivers the deal as per contract
- An evaluation report is completed

So why do companies sponsor events?

- Access target market, potential customers, age groups
- Create or enhance corporate brand image
- Build brand awareness of a product or service
- Improve customer attitude towards a product or brand
- Associate a product or service with a particular lifestyle

- Improve relationships with partners by offering a range of entertainment experiences
- Achieve product sales and merchandising opportunities
- Demonstrate new products or services
- Provide staff rewards and recognition
- Create good will, become a good corporate citizen
- Entertain key clients with corporate hospitality
- Conduct research and development
- Recruit staff

So what are we able to offer sponsors?

- Agreement to purchase sponsor's product (such as food)
- Event naming rights ("The XYZ Festival")
- "This event is sponsored by"
- Business and sponsor networking opportunities
- Merchandising rights
- Media exposure, including advertising opportunities
- Event signage
- Joint advertising with sponsors, brochure, radio and so on
- Free ticket to event
- On-site branding, stage, flags, banners
- Editorial or press releases
- Pop-up displays
- Web site or links
- Branded headed letter paper
- Event press launch
- Hospitality, VIP lounge
- Announcement, speeches, address
- Promotional giveaways
- Branded event clothing
- [X] number of tickets, passes, VIP parking
- Branded tickets, passes
- Branded bags, giveaways
- Event [XYZ] tent, lounge, room
- Inserts in goodie bags

- Competitions
- Area to display a promotional trailer or stand
- Branding in guides and listings

Seeking sponsorship can be an incredibly time-consuming activity, requiring planning, persistence and a bit of luck!

In-kind offers

Do, however, consider in-kind offers of help. No money exchanges hands but, for example, a service is provided such as a public address system in return for on-site and pre-event branding opportunities. Printers, for example, may charge you less for a print run if they can leave their logo on the leaflet. The best thing is to ask but always bear in mind that this is a business deal. The potential sponsor is ultimately thinking about whether the package on offer is good for their business.

Those who regularly obtain sponsorship understand that they need to be:

- Well researched
- Ready
- Persistent
- Realistic
- Professional
- Knowledgeable about their event numbers (such as audience number and type, quantifiable branding opportunities, number of leaflets produced and distributed)

Event legislation

NOTE: the following section does relate to the situation in the UK. However, the principles apply across other countries where similar laws or working practices are in force.

It was not that long ago that events were considered just a bit of fun, attracting little interest from the legal world. However, legislation governing how event managers should go about their business is now firmly in place. New laws (criminal and civil) and standards are added to the statute book every year. Event managers must comply with the law. It does not matter what size event you are organizing, compliance is essential. Events legislation falls into two types: criminal and civil caw:

Criminal law governs the relationship of the state with individuals where types of behaviours are set and penalties established for those who break them. For example, event managers have a statutory duty to provide a safe environment for all staff and guests.

Civil law governs the relationship between individuals in society—a "tort" or "wrong" could be the non-provision of a service and or negligent act at an event.

At any event, regardless of size or form, it is most likely that the event manager will be responsible under the Health and Safety at Work etc. Act 1974 ("the Act") for the safety and comfort of those attending the event, any employees or volunteers and contractors working on site. Employers, employees, contractors and service providers all have responsibilities under the Act. Event managers will also have contractual relationships with both suppliers and members of the public, which in the latter case is covered by the civil courts. They may also have duties to perform under Acts such as the Licensing Act 2003.

Event managers will need to be aware that, during the planning and delivery of an event, a wide range of legislation must be complied with. Some of these are specific to events; others apply to all businesses. Some create criminal offences for a breach; others are of a civil nature and govern your relationship with individuals.

These laws (Acts) are accompanied by statutory instruments or regulations, approved codes of practice and guidance notes, which set out how an employer (or event manager) can comply with the aims of the Act and the law. Generally, if you follow the available guidance for a particular activity, you will be complying with the law.

Some of the Acts that can apply to the events industry are:

- Licensing Act 2003 (please see below for further details)
- Management of Health and Safety at Work Regulations 1999 (for example, concerning risk assessments)
- Licensing (Young Persons) Act 2000 (which forbids the sale of alcohol to people under the age of 18)
- Copyright, Designs and Patents Act 1988
- Civil Contingencies Act 2004
- Private Security Industry Act 2001
- Reporting of Injuries, Diseases and Dangerous Occurrences Regulations 1995 (RIDDOR)
- Lifting Operations and Lifting Equipment Regulations 1998 (LOLER)
- Manual Handling Operations Regulations 1992
- Personal Protective Equipment at Work Regulations 1992 (PPE)
- Control of Substances Hazardous to Health Regulations 2002 (COSHH)
- Regulatory Reform (Fire Safety) Order 2005
- Control of Asbestos at Work Regulations 2002

- Display Screen Equipment Regulations 1992
- Health and Safety (First Aid) Regulations 1981
- Corporate Manslaughter and Corporate Homicide Act 2007

There is a range of consumer legislation too, and you will need you will need to be aware of some of these, including:

- Supply of Goods and Services Act 1982
- Sale of Goods (Amendment) Act 1995
- Unfair Contract Terms Act 1997

Licensing Act 2003 (UK only)

The Licensing Act 2003 amalgamated various different pieces of licensing legislation into one act. It has four objectives:

1. The prevention of crime and disorder
2. Public safety
3. The prevention of public nuisance
4. The protection of children from harm

The licensing authorities are now local councils who, dependent on the type of licence required, need to consult a variety of other organizations too. A fee will need to be paid, and certain conditions must be satisfactorily met before a licence is granted. For full local details about licences and conditions in your area, please contact your local authority. There are four types of licence:

1. The Personal Licence
2. The Premises Licence
3. The Club Premises Certificate
4. The Temporary Events Notice (up to 499 people)

You will need a licence if your event is going to include any of the following licensable activities:

- The provision of regulated entertainment for films, live music, recorded music and dance performances
- Provision of entertainment facilities for making music, dancing and entertainment of a similar description
- The sale of alcohol by retail
- The sale of hot food from 11pm to 5am

The licensing process can take anything from a few days for a Temporary Events Notice (TEN) to several months for a large outdoor event. For larger events where a licence is required, it is wise to allow yourself plenty of time to attend licensing meetings and produce all the necessary plans so you can be sure that your licence is in place, well before event day. There is a fee to pay and this will depend on the licence being requested and the amount of work the licensing authorities believe it will take to cover all the necessary requirements.

On receipt of your licence, the onus is on you and your event teams to make sure that the above licensing objectives and any local conditions imposed are met in full. You will also have to display the licence at your event.

While most corporate events will not be seeking a licence, it is worth being aware of legislation should you consider, perhaps, running an event outdoors or under canvas.

Top tip

If you are in any doubt, please seek proper advice.

Health and safety management

As you now know, as an event manager you have a legal obligation to provide a safe event. It is something you have to do. Your job is to take every reasonable precaution to ensure that your event is as safe as it can be. No person working at or visiting an event expects his or her safety to be compromised in any way. That is not to say that they cannot feel scared, nervous, excited, or think they are doing something dangerous, as part of their event experience. However, despite our best efforts, visitors may still put themselves at risk by their actions whilst on site.

The Health and Safety at Work etc. Act 1974

As previously mentioned, regardless of size or form, it is most likely that the event organizer will be responsible under The Health and Safety at Work etc. Act 1974 for the safety and comfort of those attending the event, any employees or volunteers and contractors working on site. Any duties in the Act must be carried out "so far as is reasonably practicable", meaning risks do not have to be "treated" if they are considered as almost impossibilities or if the time or cost taken to decrease the risk is greatly disproportionate to the risk itself. The Act also applies to employers, employees, contractors and service providers.

Event safety requires a partnership approach. The Act's central principle is that those responsible for creating the risk (such as event managers) have certain duties to "discharge". A summary of the Act relating to events is as follows:

- Those responsible for creating the risk have certain duties to discharge (they must do certain things)
- Event managers have a legal duty to protect the health, safety and welfare of their staff, volunteers and those attending events as well as providing services

- Service providers have similar duties
- Event venues also have similar duties, but they are not responsible for you or your audience's actions or activities while on their site (that is your responsibility)

Trying to ensure that you have taken every reasonable safety precaution can feel like an onerous and lonely task. Please, however, avoid using health and safety as an excuse for not running an event. Health and safety laws do not ban or stop events; event managers and officials do. If you seek good advice or think creatively about how you can deliver a safe event that is still exciting, there should be no health and safety issues to prevent your event from being successful.

Event insurance

All events must carry an appropriate level of insurance cover, so you MUST check to see exactly what cover you or your organization already have in place. Ask the difficult questions: you need to know what you are or are *not* covered for. Never assume anything!

The three key polices relating to events are as follows:

- Public liability
- Product liability
- Employers' liability

Other general insurance policies relevant to events and event managers are:

- Non-appearance (when a key person does not turn up)
- All risks and equipment hire (typically covering loss or damage to goods hired to you)

- Cancellation, abandonment, postponement (covering actual event costs and sometimes income lost)
- Damage to event (covering damage to a venue before, during or after the event)
- Rain (covering income lost through reduced ticket sales because of rain, plus costs already incurred)
- Event-specific policies (such as fireworks, street parties, exhibitions)
- Multiple events (as the name suggests, covering for 15 or more events a year)
- Prize indemnity (financial reimbursement for prize pay-out)
- Professional indemnity or liability (consequences of poor advice)

You will not require all of these policies to be in place every time you organize an event. As a basic minimum, you will need public, employers' and (if you intend to sell products) product liability cover.

I would also recommend all risks and equipment insurance if you intend to hire any high-value equipment. It is also worth considering other risks that your event may face, such as the loss of the key sponsor or strategic partner and poor ticket sales. What would happen to your event if any of these occurred? Could you still run your event?

Top tip

All other contractors, performers, speakers, caterers and so on need their own insurance too. You will need to request copies of all policies to ensure they are current and valid.

In summary

- Pay great attention to the detail.
- Always have actions in your event project plan based on reviewing the progress of the plan and, for example, on reviewing the financial commitments to date.
- Try to create "continuous urgency". Make sure all of your event team meetings move the event forward and do not stall it (until the next meeting). You need decisions, not more chat.
- In terms of making sure you always have a productive day, think about "Do lists"; pick the most important daily tasks and prioritise them 1, 2 and 3. They are better than "To do" lists (or, more aptly, "Not to do").
- Something that helps me on a daily basis is making sure I attend to the biggest, most important (and sometimes most scary) task first in the morning. Get that done and the rest of the day feels like a breeze.
- Other things that will help you include knowing the difference between important and urgent tasks, being brave enough to switch off the email while doing important tasks, and understanding that today is not over until you have planned tomorrow.
- Select your contractors, speakers, entertainment and exhibitors wisely. Do they all have the right level of insurance and have you seen a copy of it?
- Time spent getting the right people on board is always time well spent.
- The budget has to be determined with the event objective in mind—a bold objective requires a big budget.
- Know your figures—know where the budget is being spent and where the money is being made.
- The success of your event will depend entirely upon the effort, care and skill you apply in its planning.
- Ensuring everybody's health and safety is not optional. It is a must-do. Take good advice and work with competent and experienced people.

CHAPTER 5

PLACES: CREATING THE PERFECT EVENT VENUE

Finding the right venue for your conference, exhibition, talk or dinner—or making the best use of your own—is one of the most important considerations when organizing an event. The right venue, and the way it is laid out, really does set the tone of your event and the sense of occasion. Think: event first, venue second.

The three key factors determining whether your venue is the right choice are:

1. Should the host organisation, partners, sponsors—be using that venue?
2. The event programme—would the venue suit your activities, speakers, workshops, entertainment?
3. The audience—would they like being there?

To start, you need to decide your venue search criteria. The following will help you decide what your key venue criteria should be:

- Location—region, country, "wow", quiet, city centre, rural
- Transport—good public and road links, airport
- Busy, exclusive use, iconic
- Does the venue need to match the event's style and sense of occasion?
- Size and type (indoor or outdoor) of space required, people, installations
- Event size, numbers visiting—occupant capacity, numbers staying
- Duration and timing of event
- A blank canvas, best fit, build-your-own, pre-themed
- Does it need to have an environmental policy?

Once you have agreed your venue criteria, you can begin a more structured search for the right venue.

Venue occupant capacity

It is crucial that you know the number of people you can legally allow into your event. This figure is one of your first considerations. All reputable venues will be able to tell you how many people you can fit into each space or room. They will also be able to tell you how, when the room or space is arranged in a different format, the figures will be different. For example, if you have a drinks reception, you can fit more people into a space than if you are setting it up for a sit-down dinner. Again, good venues will be able to show a site plan of the room or space indicating the different formats possible and their respective occupant capacities.

However, if you intend to create an enclosed outdoor area for your event, you will need to work out how many people you can invite. The Health and Safety Executive (HSE) says the following in its Event Safety Guide:

"The occupant capacity is the maximum number of people who can be safely accommodated at the venue. In the case of standing areas at longer events, there is a need to take into account "sitting down" space for the audience and freedom of movement for access to toilets and refreshment facilities. It is essential to agree the occupant capacity with the local authority and fire authority as early as possible as the means of escape arrangements are dependent on this figure."

The HSE goes on to say:

"In areas where seating is provided, the major part of the occupant capacity will be determined by the number of seats available. However, in other cases, a calculation will need to be made and this is based on each person occupying an area of 0.5 m^2 [metres squared]. The maximum number of people who can be accommodated can therefore be calculated by dividing the total area available to the audience (in m^2) by 0.5."

This is the type of calculation you will need to make for a large-scale event, typically a music event. It is unlikely that you will need to know this figure for an open access family fun day or fete.

The HSE gives an example:

"[A]n outdoor site measuring 100 x 50 m with all areas available to the audience [a totally clear site] could accommodate a maximum of 10 000 people (i.e. 100 x 50 m = 5000 m^2 divided by 0.5 = 10 000)."

However, the local or fire authority may decide that for certain events this figure will need to be less.

Event venue evaluation: indoor venues

Having created a shortlist of venues that match your venue criteria, it is time to evaluate the best venue for your event. The following is a general indoor venue evaluation checklist:

- What is the location like—is it easy to find, well signed, does it need to be peaceful, or near a town centre?
- What is the geography of the area—what is the venue's proximity to major roads, airports, public transport routes, car parking, natural features such as lakes and rivers?
- Is the venue clean and tidy
- Have a look round the venue's local neighbourhood— does your event fit into the local culture and services?
- Does the venue match the event's style and sense of occasion?
- What is the venue's occupant capacity? (Each space or room is likely to have e different figure.)
- What venue facilities or services (such as tables, chairs, tablecloths, risers, podiums, lecterns, flipcharts, screens, projectors, and PA system) are available to you?
- Is there access for unloading large items into rooms or spaces (such as for a car)?
- Is there time to set up or rehearse (or both)—do you have built in sufficient time to allow for previous occupier delays?
- How soon do you need to have broken down and cleared the site before the next occupier arrives?

- Do you have exclusive use of the venue, and access times?
- Are staff experienced—are they helpful, flexible and have they handled similar occasions?
- What is the quality of food and service—for example, do the serving and catering staff have experience, is there a range of options, how many kitchens are there, do you need a licence?
- Is the room layout suitable—are there possibilities or limiting factors, is there space for displays?
- Consider "clashes" with other guests at break times and lunch
- Ensure adequate emergency plans and exits
- What about on-site communications—phones, office space and so on?
- Is it easy to get around—for the audience, contractors and staff?
- Is there any signage—inside and outside?
- Does it provide audiovisual equipment and support—in house, or can you hire your own?
- Does the venue have a preferred list of suppliers, or any exclusivity clauses?
- Are there sufficient blackout facilities for presentations, if required?
- Where can you access power?
- Are there any limiting factors—like pillars, columns and ceiling height?
- Will there be other events at the venue, clashes of culture, noise from adjoining rooms—can the venue cope?
- Is the venue free for the duration of the event—including set-up and dismantling?
- What are the sizes and types of spaces available to you?
- Do the various spaces work well together—in terms of proximity and access between them?

- Are the rooms adequately soundproofed?
- Are the rooms adequately lit—with natural or artificial light? Can you adjust it and or are their blinds/curtains if it is too bright.
- Are their sufficient electrical points on stage and or around for mobile/ tablet charging stations
- Are the rooms' air conditioned and can it be adjusted on request.
- What is the access to any outside space(s) like?
- Can you get a detailed plan of every room, if required?
- Can you establish a day rate for pricing, and exactly what it includes?
- Is there a supply of brochures and maps to send to participants, if it is a nice venue?
- What is the car parking like—in terms of location, access, charges and availability, and can you reserve car parking spaces for speakers and key guests?
- Can you find out any local transport details—such as the cost of a taxi to the nearest station?
- Is there a copy of the emergency procedure?
- Are any refurbishments planned?
- For hotels, how good is the check-in procedure? What are the interactions like between staff and guests in these areas, from your guests' point of view?
- Is there sufficient space to set up registration desks outside your event or room?
- What is the quality and level of security, if appropriate? Will your delegates be able to freely enter/ leave the venue? Are there security procedures
- What sort of catering is there—can the in-house team or contractor cope with the numbers, timings and style of catering required, and what arrangements are available for feeding your event team and contractors?
- What is the number and location of the venue's toilets, when are they cleaned and by whom?

- Can the venue staff cope with the extra numbers of people and enquiries that your event will bring?
- Is there internet or Wi-Fi access—and if so, what is the signal strength like on site, do you require a certain bandwidth to stream your event live? (Always seek appropriate advice from the venue or a specialist, or both.)
- Can you get clarification on what dates are currently available?
- Do they have any suitable availability

Searching for the perfect outdoor event venue

It is vitally important that you really understand what an outdoor venue can and cannot do. A proper venue evaluation must be completed, and should include the following:

- What is the location like—is it easy to find, well signed, does it need to be peaceful, or near a town centre?
- What is the geography of the area—what is the venue's proximity to major roads, hospitals, public transport routes, car parking, natural features such lakes and rivers?
- Does the venue match the event's style and sense of occasion?
- What is the venue's capacity and where are the exit routes?
- What is the venue's access like—can all your suppliers, traders and emergency services easily access the site?
- Is it suitable—is it the right place, can you use it safely, is it easy to use?
- What are the entrances like—will there be enough space for audiences to queue safely?

- What are the sight lines like—are there any permanent pillars or columns affecting the view of the performances?
- What is the viewing area like—how big a viewing area can you create, and are there other options?
- What are the ground conditions like—are there any slopes, is it firm under foot and what is it like when it rains?
- What effect does the weather (mainly rain) have on the venue?
- Where are the services on site, how many are there and how available are they—for water, electricity, lighting, on-site communications systems and on-site toilets?
- Is the site easily accessible to everyone who would want to attend—and if it is not, what can you do about it?
- What are the on-site parking arrangements and capacities—are there any nearby temporary car parking options?
- What will the impact be on the local community, for example from extra traffic movements, nuisance parking, rubbish and noise, and how close are nearby houses—is it possible to satisfy the needs of the audience and the neighbours?
- Can you get clarification on what dates are currently available?

Please note that, if you are using grounds or a venue owned by a local authority, you will have to fill in a form asking for permission to use an outdoor space—so make sure you find out, in good time, how long this process might take.

Venue finding services

If you do not have time to find a site for your event, a venue-finding agency may be useful—and because they charge the venue, their services to you will be free. Also, talk to your local tourist board or local authority about rooms and spaces to hire in the area. Venue-finding services are more geared up to finding venues for business events and private functions, as opposed to outdoor events.

Conducting a venue site visit

If you have a selection of possible venues to choose from, go and visit them using the above checklist to structure a site visit meeting with the venue manager. Where possible, take along a colleague, friend or other interested party, as you will be amazed at what somebody else sees that you do not. The following may also help get the best out of your site visit.

Stop

- Give the venue your full concentration
- Compile a list of questions—use the event venue evaluation checklist as a guide

Look

- Consider if it is attractive and looked after well, and if it reaches a good standard of cleanliness
- Try to visualize your event taking place there and take photographs
- Look everywhere inside and outside that is relevant
- Think about the set-up and break-down
- Ask to see a Health and Safety Plan

Listen

- Are all the venue's staff polite and courteous?
- Are all your questions being answered to your satisfaction?

- Do you get the impression that they are genuinely interested in helping you deliver a great event? (Being able to build up a strong relationship with the venue manager will make such a difference when you require changes on or near event day.)
- Meet the venue's event day team. Can you work with them?

Event venue quotes

Consider the following:

- Hire costs for a room, the rates for a part-day, all day or per head, or for land hire, and make sure you know exactly what you are getting for your money
- Costs of all food, drinks rates and related service charges
- Costs of all other items and services hired by or provided to you
- Written quotes, with or without VAT
- Repayment schedule, such as a deposit to secure the site or payment in full, up front or after the event

Once you are satisfied with the figures (which should be supplied in writing) and you can picture your event working there, make a provisional booking with the venue as soon as you can. When you are entirely happy with the detail, confirm your booking in writing. It is highly likely that, at this point, you will be required to sign a contract with the venue. On signing the contract, you will have to pay a deposit (to secure the booking) and, for outdoor events also damage deposit (to cover the cost of any reinstatement work required because of your use of the facility).

I offered general advice about contracts in Chapter 4, but here are a few other points to remember about your venue contract:

1. Review it to check, for example, that all the dates and details match up to your expectations
2. Clarify certain clauses to make sure you know, for example, the minimum numbers that your pricing schedule has been based on and what might happen if you do not achieve this number of attendees. Would you have to pay the difference? (This is often known as an "attrition clause".)
3. Check whether the venue would guarantee room rate prices, menu pricing and so on
4. Make sure you know whether the cancellation period is based on days or working days (ensure it is working days)
5. As a general rule, remove all exclusivity clauses, such as those relating to audiovisual suppliers. Removing these clauses will give you more choice. (You may indeed end up using the in-house supplier but, without an exclusivity clause, you can at least check out other companies to see how they compare.)
6. Check cancellation charges to see if the venue will be charging you any interest and, if so, what the rate will be
7. Clarify what constitutes, in the venue's opinion, a breach of contract
8. Do check to make sure you are allowed to use the venue's logo on any of your event publicity
9. Do make sure all amendments to the contract are completed to your satisfaction and a new typed copy is forwarded to you to sign and return

Planning your event site: the site plan

Even for a small event, a simple plan is a necessity, obviating the need for detailed explanations while you are trying to set the site up. It can also help to identify possible problem areas. The general principle when creating an event site plan is to ensure the layout allows your room, marquee or space to feel comfortably full, with room to circulate, move around and, if relevant, be served.

When creating the site plan, the event manager will need to consider:

- Audience safety
- Creating an arena where the audience can see or take part in the entertainment or programme
- Reducing the impact that your event has on the general environment (such as traffic movements, noise, litter)

The following list will help you plan your site. You will need to locate or consider all or some of the following:

- Emergency exits and access routes
- Staffing positions, roles, numbers
- Event control point
- First aid position
- Waste management
- Toilets and their location(s)
- Catering
- Entrances and exits, where to queue
- Speaker position
- Themed props
- Audiovisual equipment and production position
- Structures, such as stages, marquees, gazebos
- Stage or performance area (or both)
- Traders

- Sight lines, making sure everybody can see the performance, stage and speakers
- Location of key event signage
- Noise considerations, including location of speakers and direction in which the stage is pointing
- Position of any temporary power sources, (such as a generator)
- Reception and registration areas
- Information area
- Layout of room(s), space(s), table(s)

Where possible, try to get a digital map of your whole site, enlarge it to A3 size, photocopy it and then draw your plan onto it in pencil, as things will change. If you can, try drafting your site plan roughly to scale. You will, therefore, need accurate dimensions from anything that is out of the ordinary, such as an exhibition stand or demonstration area. For outdoor events, it is also worth creating a wet weather "contingency" site plan, just in case parts of your site are prone to flooding and become waterlogged. So do make a point of visiting outdoor venues when it is raining or just after a period of heavy rain. It could help to improve your site planning, removing the need to make wholesale event day changes should it rain.

In summary

- Please remember: "event first, venue second", so be creative in your venue choice, when you can.
- Find a best-fit venue first, before you recreate your event space from scratch.
- When you visit a venue, take as long as you feel you need. If you are not sure, go back again. It is an important decision and not one to take lightly. But do not take too long as somebody else may book it while you are thinking about it.

- If you are using your own venue, please be sure you evaluate it properly too. Know its limitations.
- Final venue costs will be a factor of the result you want: if you want the best experience, the best food, exclusivity and so on, it will come at a price.
- Never take it for granted that you will get permission to use a local authority venue. Do seek the correct approvals. Your choice of event venue and its performance on event day will have a huge bearing on the ultimate success of your event. If the venue does not live up to your audience's expectations, they will blame the event manager, not the venue!

CHAPTER 6

PROGRAMME: CREATING MUST-SEE EVENT PROGRAMMES

The event programme outlines what your audience is going to do, take part in, listen to, watch and eat. It can make or break an event. Some would say that it is the most important component of any event because it is generally the reason why your audience is there. If you want your audience to remember your event programme for all the right reasons, it has to be exciting, interesting, engaging, enjoyable and memorable. For events such as launches, seminars and conferences, your event programme should contain moments of "you heard it here first": little nuggets of advice or information or "ah ha!" moments.

The event programme is the schedule of activities, entertainment, speakers and catering over a set period. It is constructed much like a play, scene by scene. Each element of the programme is carefully considered by the event manager in terms of its impact, relevance and time taken. In an ideal world, the event programme should flow from one thing to another with occasional breaks for people to catch their breath.

The key factors to consider when you planning your event programme are as follows:

- What you want to achieve
- What your audience will be interested in and want to know about
- What you want your audience to think, feel or learn
- Venue constraints, what you can actually do at the venue, and any venue rules
- Whether you or your team (or both) have the skills and experience to make it work
- Do your research to find out what is "hip and happening" Ask questions – never assume audience knowledge
- If you are using a theme, ensure the programme reflects it
- Find a way of telling people stories; they are very powerful. They can illustrate the struggle between expectation and reality; they create a much more emotional response and are therefore more impactful. They are often your social proof demonstrating your services or products actually do work.
- Presentations, ideally a combination of words, images and video with few numbers.
- The agenda should be based on value, presence and interest but not seniority
- Create a pull for leadership; we want to hear what they thought of the speakers and not just listen to the prepared speech they wrote a few days ago
- Try to ensure that your programme is varied and engaging to avoid your delegates' natural lows
- Consider whether you want the event programme streamed live, which will require thought, money and a contractor, or whether you will make the presentations available to delegates via email or the event web site
- Pre-conditioning. Before your delegates or guests arrive for the event you may want to send them something to

do or listen to: a video, some questions, a task . . . to get them in the right frame of mind.

Event programming

Your event programme can be made up of any number of the following items:

- Speakers—business, motivational, after-dinner, comedians
- Street entertainment, theatre, cabaret, shows
- Any kind of workshop
- Photographic displays, illustrations, art works
- Special effects, fireworks, lasers, large-scale projection
- Mass participatory activities or parades
- Presentations, lectures, interactive question-and-answer sessions
- Demonstrations, seminars
- Static exhibitions, traders
- Games, competitions, tournaments, taster sessions, competitions, videos
- Music of any description, whether discos, musicals, background or interval music
- Mix-and-mingle entertainment, such as close-up magic, children's entertainment, adult entertainment, celebrities
- Outdoor attractions, including those you can hire, like ice rinks, funfairs, extreme sports activities
- And, of course, consider what they are going to eat!

Always ask yourself whether the chosen activity fits the space, occasion and time. Also consider if it is likely to leave the audience wanting more, not wishing for less. Where possible, you should try to build a varied programme that has changes of tempo, style and format built in.

Encouraging audience participation

Most event audiences are, in the main, an outgoing bunch, so the words "audience participation" should not make them come out in a cold sweat. Encouraging your audiences to get involved in the event is actually good for them. When audiences start to feel part of an event, they can get a real sense of engagement—leaving with great memories and a strong impression of the event organizers. So, how are you going to involve your audience? What are they going to take part in, learn, decide, experience or solve?

You can encourage involvement and interactivity with:

- Taster, "have a go" sessions
- Creative thinking sessions
- Quizzes
- Games, competitions, tournaments
- Debates, problem-solving sessions, panels
- Small to large, or mass participatory activities
- Practical demonstrations
- Workshops, talks, shows
- Voting, rating systems
- Peer-to-peer sessions, "round table" topic-based discussion with peers

Remember the well-known proverb: "Tell me and I will forget, show me and I may remember, involve me and I will understand." How true this is to the world of event programming. Make your audience really feel part of your event.

Finalising your event programme

With a clear idea of what you would like to include in your programme, you now need to finalise it, so:

- List and cost all items you intend to include in the programme
- Establish what you know about each programme item, such as time, layout, turnover times and set-up, and consider cost versus value
- Set all the activity timings and determine exactly how long each item will last. Allow for a small degree of flexibility when organizing your event timetable
- Know that each item fits the space, time, audience, sponsor, client and budget
- Work out whether there is a logical order they should follow
- Be clear in your own mind that each item does what you intended it to do and enhances the event
- Draft up the programme, walk through it in your own mind, take it to a test panel (potential audience members), get their feedback
- Modify and confirm the programme
- Send a contract or agreement to all programme participants
- Where appropriate, ask for short biographies from the key acts for your printed programme or web site (or both)
- Design, proof and print the event programme brochure. It should contain front and back cover (logos, sponsors, cost), welcome, contents page, programme of the day (times, venue, cost), house rules or requests, sponsors' adverts and a note to say "thank you for coming"
- Decide which elements of the programme you want to make available to delegates after the event and how

(such as emailed to everyone or available for download from the event web site)

Note: do not forget to send everyone involved in your event a very detailed set of joining instructions (see Chapter 8, Production) to include maps, significant landmarks and written instructions.

Booking a great speaker

Ideally, a great speaker brings an immediate emotional and mental connection, a stage presence and an energy, which captivates and lights up the whole auditorium. Their primary job has to be to delight, inspire, engage and entertain as well as inform the audience. Nobody wants to listen to speeches that the speakers do not want to give, or to sit through dreary obligatory talks. Audiences want to listen to people who are excited to be speaking. Therefore, select your speakers wisely and carefully. There is a lot at stake.

Here are a few thoughts on selecting your speaker(s):

- Can you meet them or audition them on the phone? How do you feel when speaking to them on the phone— excited, interested . . . you need to be.
- Do they listen?
- Do you like them?
- Do they understand what you are trying to do?
- Do their ideas fit your event theme?
- Are they persuasive? Do they grab your attention?
- Can they communicate powerfully in a direct and simple way?
- Do you think you can work with this person?
- Have you talked to others they have worked with? What do they think?

- Has anyone actually heard them give a speech at an event? What do they think?
- Have you at least seen them on a video?
- Can you have a look at the slides from a sample presentation?
- Do they give speeches at many events like yours?
- Do they speak well of other contributors?
- Are they rigid or accommodating?
- Do they have a sense of humour?
- Do they have an agent representing them?
- Have you searched the web using the speaker's name to see what others are saying about them or if they have been quoted in the press? (Remember: your guests may well do similar research.)
- Do they have a high profile on the web?
- In conversation with them do you get a sense that they really care about your audience and want to help them?

On a more practical note, please ensure that you know what type and version of software the speaker will use. Those responsible for providing your technical and presentational equipment need this information in advance. You should also ask all speakers to send you their presentation prior to the event, so you can check that it works. They must also bring a copy of it with them on a memory stick as back-up.

Finding a great speaker

There are a number of speaker agencies with a whole raft of different types of speakers on their books, from business leaders and politicians to actors, adventurers and sportspeople. There are also good speakers who appear at local events and networking meetings and who may come free. Ask around, talk to associations like the Chambers of Commerce and attend business expos: you will be surprised just how many good non-professional speakers there are on the circuit. You can of course search the internet as well.

Booking a master of ceremonies or conference moderator

Many of the key requirements of a good speaker also apply to the master of ceremonies. The key requirement is that they can quickly form a rapport with your audience, command the attention of an audience, understand the boundaries of operating in a public arena and know when to pass on information and when to be quiet! They need to have poise and presence and the ability to adjust or ad lib as necessary.

A conference moderator introduces all the speakers or activities and links them all together, often passing comment on the previous speaker before introducing the next one. They can also be used as a panel chair, for example to pose questions and tease out answers. They link the whole programme together. There are professional conference moderators, or a senior member of staff can undertake the role.

Correctly introducing the speakers is a skill. The purpose of the speaker introductions is threefold:

1. To grab hold of the audience's attention
2. To entice the audience to pay attention, understand why they need to listen
3. To build up the credibility of the speaker

A good master of ceremonies can really lift an event. They are, in effect, the genial host and conductor ensuring that the programme (with the assistance of the event manager) runs smoothly and on time. Ensure that your master of ceremonies has impeccable credentials.

Tips on how to deliver the perfect presentation

As you will no doubt have discovered, not all speakers or presentations are equal. All speaker presentations should, however, leave us wishing for more and not less. We should not feel the need to check our emails while we wait for something interesting to be said.

Here are a few presentation tips and techniques that will help your speakers to deliver the perfect presentation:

- The presentation title—bold, about the audience's most-wanted outcome
- Know why you are talking—your audience must learn something
- Know how long you can speak for and stick to it—rehearse accordingly, time yourself and then edit the copy; the more confident you get, the longer you will take
- Introduce yourself—tell your audience why you are able to stand there and talk to them, why you are the expert
- Have a killer opening statement
- The programme—list the things you are going to talk about
- Cover only one point at a time—no multi-tasking when it comes to attention; we only pay attention to one thing at a time, or one point per slide
- Use patterns—we remember them better than details
- After every 10 to 15 minutes, your audience will start to fade; tell them a story, do an exercise or ask a question
- We learn a lot more through pictures (it is our dominant sense) than through the spoken word; incorporate images into your presentation wherever you can

- Mannerisms—know what you do and, in some cases, stop doing them
- Seeding—let the audience know what is coming up
- Summarise—periodically summarise the key points and check for understanding
- Avoid too much animation, changes in font size or fonts
- Make sure all video clips, for example, actually have the video file inserted into the slide
- Tone of voice—loud, quiet, change of tempo; keep it interesting
- Make eye contact—a few seconds per person per point
- Use silence—it is very powerful and gives the audience a little thinking time
- Be relevant, honest and current—keep it real and make them laugh
- Use the senses—the big picture, imagine if you could, hear what they will be saying
- Limit the use of numbers
- Watch your stance—steady middle ground, not too much arm action; when you move, do it with purpose to make a new point
- Tell people stories in colour, in lots of detail. Stories create a much more emotional response and are therefore more impactful.
- Tap into people's emotions and fears
- Deck your presentation out with audio, video, pictures
- Ask your audience "yes" questions—so they all feel that it is for them
- Red thread—keep referring back to the theme of your talk
- Evidence—provide statistics and facts to confirm that what you are saying works and is true
- Big finish—try to sum up with a memorable line

- Speak at 120 words per minute, not the usual 160 words per minute for conversations

You can, of course, prepare a presentation "tips sheet" and send it to all your speakers before the event to help them get it right on the day. This could be particularly helpful if you are booking non-professional speakers

Social events: booking acts, entertainment and activities

While most corporate events are a combination of speakers and workshops, you may want to lighten the programme a little by adding some acts or entertainment, something a little different. You may also be planning a social aspect of your event.

The following booking entertainment checklist will guide you through the process of searching, selecting and contracting the right acts and entertainment:

- Why do you need entertainment?
- What entertainment do you need?
- Where do you need entertainers?
- When do you need entertainers?
- How long do you need the entertainers for?
- What time do you want entertainers on site?
- How long do they take to set up and break down?
- Do they have any accompanying personnel—numbers, needs, roles?
- What is their availability for rehearsal?
- What will they do or not do for the media?
- What requirements do you know they have—space, technical, safety, hotel, transport, parking?

- Do they have references, are they vetted, are they members of an appropriate association or talent group?
- Back-up plan—what will you do in the event of equipment failure, non-appearance, sickness?
- When do you want them to leave?
- How much will it cost, what is the agreed percentage of takings or earning potential?
- When and how will they need paying?
- Do they have a contract (agent) or other legal conditions (or both)?
- Have you seen all necessary risk assessments and insurance certifications?

Booking a DJ

DJs are the ideal option for any social event lacking the budget or space required to hire a live band. Whilst not always as fun to watch as a band, quality DJs offer a high level of interaction with audiences and can keep a dance floor packed all night.

When booking a DJ, consider the following:

- Quality—are they reliable and recommended, do they carry professional equipment and have considerable experience of events like yours, can they provide a low-budget show with a small amount of equipment right up to a large show incorporating equipment such as video projectors, large sound systems, elaborate lighting shows and live dancers?
- Style of music and song list—does their play list suit your taste and fit the tone of your occasion?
- Can they give you a sample play list?
- Experience—a good quality function DJ will be experienced and have many previous engagements

under their belt; do they have references to ensure that their experience and showmanship is well above average?

- Equipment—DJs can carry quite an array of equipment to functions, ranging from small mixing decks, CD and mini-disk players, and computer systems to quite large sound systems and disco lighting; what do they have by way of back-up should any equipment fail?
- Cost—when booking a DJ, it is important to understand that you get what you pay for; are the DJs in demand and do they command higher fees than newer or inexperienced DJs who may have a starter-range of equipment?
- Space—is there enough space for a DJ, their equipment and a dance floor, and are these near to a source of power?

Booking a band

There is nothing better than great live entertainment. It can really make a great social event. To get this element of your event right, here is a list of things to think about when booking live entertainment:

- Book early—the best live bands will be booked up to nine months in advance
- Confirm that your venue allows live music and, if so, are there any specific conditions?
- Check your choice of live band—are they right for the audience and venue?
- Sign contracts—secure your band before someone else books them and read the agent's or band's terms and conditions of booking very carefully

Upon signing your contract, you will need to confirm:

- Full venue address
- Contact name and number for the event manager and venue
- Exact date of event
- Band arrival, sound check, performance and finish times

You will need to know the following:

- Band name and contact number or agent's details (or both)
- Provision of trolleys or helpers for the band if load-in includes stairs or if the performance area is over 50 metres away from the delivery point
- Band size and space required
- Whether you need to provide or create a good-sized dance floor
- Whether there is an electricity supply for the band
- Whether you need to book a changing room for the band
- If you need to arrange the band's "rider"—special requests over and above the contract, such as mileage, drinks, hot meal
- Performance start and finish times—in some cases, finish times are not negotiable; your licence conditions say so
- If you need to create a play list (if you want to)
- Preferred dress code (if required)—specify to the band or their agent what attire will be most fitting for the band to wear at your event
- Payment method—how and when, VAT registration, and so on

You should also:

- arrange to meet the band on arrival and allocate one person to be the band liaison throughout, able to deal with noise issues, minor complaints and over-enthusiastic guests
- arrange set-up and a sound-check time to ensure agreeable volume levels and to discuss the use of any smoke machines, strobe lighting, and so on
- keep the band updated—especially if the event runs behind schedule; most bands are very flexible about changes to start times but they may need to alter their show if performance lengths need to be changed

DJs or live entertainment can make or break a great party or dinner. You must do your research and get the best you can afford. There are also great local bands who charge a much more modest fee; the problem lies in finding them and being convinced that they will do a good job for you.

Performance spaces and stages

The chances are that you will book a speaker, act or entertainer or arrange some kind or performance. You will, therefore, need to create a performance area. Your first priority is to establish how big an area they need and whether they have any special requirements. At this point, it is worth establishing the activity's "must-have" items from the "would-like-to-have" items. In terms of the performance space, this can be as simple as providing an appropriately-sized area or the use of an existing stage. The floor is fine too if your guests are sitting down. In fact, all kinds of structures can become a performance area. You can simply lay a rope on the floor to indicate where people need to stand or sit.

More substantive performance spaces are created by linking together an appropriate number of staging blocks. These staging blocks or systems often start at a height of about 15 to 16 centimetres and can be increased incrementally up to several metres in height for larger-scale events. As the stage gets higher, you will be required to have safety barriers (on the back and sides) as well as steps or a ramp (or both). The ramp is to allow large heavy items of equipment to be wheeled onto the stage. In this case, you will need to consider hiring a reputable staging company who will know the current regulations regarding staging, barriers, steps and ramps.

You may also need to provide a covered performance space if you are outdoors. There are really only two ways of doing this:

1. A covered standalone stage—provided by a staging company
2. A stage or performance space created inside a marquee; in this case, you will need to consider all the relevant fire and safety risks and take appropriate action; in the case of the marquee, you will need to determine how many people you can fit in it, as it is now effectively an indoor venue (so it is worth taking professional advice)

Booking traders, stall holders and exhibitors

At certain types of events, it is also likely that you may want to invite organizations to come and exhibit at your event. As with everyone else providing services or working at your event, the usual rules apply concerning risk assessment and insurance, even for the smallest of displays or stands. You cannot afford to take the risk, however unlikely you may think it is. You could also invite traders and stallholders to your event, not only to add a little variety to your event but also to generate some income. In this case, you may want to create a food court or trade area.

So what do you need to do?

Firstly, decide whether you have the space and resources to administer the process of finding, checking and managing any traders and exhibitors while on site.

Secondly, and more importantly, do consider whether having traders and exhibitors enhances your event or just the income figure on your budget sheet. Before you start looking for exhibitors, traders and stallholders, consider the following:

- Do you have the space? If so, how much space do you have and what percentage of the available space are you happy to turn over to traders and exhibitors?
- What sort of exhibitors, traders or stallholders do you want? (Ideally, it should be organizations that actually look like they should be there; in other words, they "fit in" with your event's theme and original purpose.)
- What sort of fee do you charge? After all, you are providing them with an audience of potential buyers; you could charge a pre-agreed percentage of their overall "take"; I would recommend that you charge a fixed up-front payment, and then you will have your money whatever happens on event day. (Remember: this is money in the bank; pitch fees can start at anything from £5 to several £1,000's.)
- The whole process of administering traders and exhibitors is time-consuming and often a little frustrating! Do you have somebody in mind who has the time and determination to manage the process?

A word to the wise: please do not just sign up everybody who contacts you; be selective and consider whether they are the right sort of trader for your event.

The trade pack

The trade or exhibitor pack is the information you send out to trade enquirers, and it should contain the following:

- Overview of your event—a few words that encapsulate the essence of your event
- Event date
- Event opening times
- Public ticket prices (if appropriate)
- Details of the event's promotional campaign
- Details of the organizers and their contact points
- Description of the exhibition trade space, like floor space, marquee, hall
- Pitch sizes and prices, early-bird offers if they book before a certain date
- Type of pitch—what can you provide them with, such as table, chairs, power or cover? (You are not required to provide them with anything but you can choose to if you feel it would be helpful.)
- Car and van parking arrangements—will there be any on-site parking or will they need to go to a designated parking area once they have unloaded and set up?
- Set-up times—when will you allow them on site to set up, by what time must they be set up, and by what time must they remove all vehicles
- Trading times
- Break-down times
- Venue details
- Audience numbers and profile—do not lie to them (as you will have to deal with the consequences!)

- Larger marquee pitches
- Booking deadline, joining instructions
- Booking form

It should also contain general booking conditions, such as:

- Confirmed bookings—these will only be accepted once full payment and all the appropriate paperwork have been received
- Exclusive right—the granting of trade space does not guarantee the trader sole right of selling or promoting their particular commodity or service unless the organizers approve such an agreement in writing
- Right to refuse—the event organizers reserve the right to refuse any application without explanation
- Sale item—your booking will be taken based on the information given; you will not be able to display or sell items not listed or which the organizer feels to be inappropriate
- Cancellation by exhibitor or trader—should they wish to withdraw a confirmed application for any reason, there will be a cancellation or administration fee of 25% of the total site fee; there will no refunds given for cancellations made within 15 days of the event
- Certificates and insurance—as part of the condition of entry, all traders must hold and send with their application form copies of their public, product and employers' liability insurances; all food producers must also enclose a copy of their local authority registration details and their food hygiene certificates
- Risk assessment—all exhibitors and traders must also complete a full risk assessment

Traders, stall holders and exhibitors can be a very valuable source of income and interest at events. However, the process of finding, administering and managing them while on site will always be time-consuming. Alas, not all of them will do exactly what you want them to do: they will delay payment and not send in booking forms, risk assessments and insurance details. They just might buy the wrong pitch size—the smaller, cheaper one—and then want you to find them a bigger pitch, but not pay for the upgrade. As with the real world of events, some events will be more successful than others. Consequently, your traders will have good days and bad days and probably have an event day demeanour to match!

Event catering

Most corporate events offer some form of catering. The style and extent of which will be largely dependent on how much you have to spend and the type of event being planned. At certain types of corporate events, it is worth spending a little extra on catering to ensure that you offer the best food you can afford. Delegates, as previously mentioned in this chapter, have signed up based on what they are going to learn or take part in and who they are going to meet (the programme) and not what they are going to eat.

Clearly, if you are trying to impress, then your food needs to impress too. If you have an event theme, you may wish to try theming your food offering accordingly. Try renaming dishes to tie in with your theme and consider creating bespoke dishes where possible. You can choose to offer any of the following:

- A la carte—anything off the menu
- Set menu
- Cold or hot buffet
- Sandwiches
- BBQ
- Picnics

- Cocktail reception
- Canapés
- Breakfast
- Bowl food
- Reception drinks
- Drinks only
- Free bar or pay bar
- Breakfast, lunch, dinner, afternoon tea

There are also wide selections of mobile catering units offering a range of foods.

The important things to consider when providing any sort of catering at your events include:

- Have in mind what you consider an acceptable budget for food
- Decide how many people you think you are catering for, including staff
- Consider just how important the food is to the overall success of your event
- Think about what your audience might be expecting for the ticket price and what they might need
- Think about the style of catering you want to offer, set against the cost of providing or serving it (or both)
- Always request an extra table so guests can put their dirty plates on it, or ensure there are plenty of staff to clear away. (There is nothing worse than seeing piles of dirty plates and napkins lying around your catering areas; if you were having a meal in a restaurant, you would expect to have your plates cleared after each course, and events are no different.)
- Consider if you want the venue's bar open. Will the venue want you pay for the staff and keep the takings, and how many bar staff will they need to cope with any peak event demand?

- Seek clarification on all the charges that you will incur relating to the catering, bar, clearing staff, and glass and crockery hire
- Do you need to secure a licence to sell alcohol?

Further practical issues to consider

There is no doubting that some of your guests will place a higher than fair store on the quality of the food at your event, even if the events are free to attend. It therefore pays to be honest in all your event's promotional material. If you are only providing sandwiches, say so. I often use the words "light refreshments will be provided" at many of my events. This cannot be misinterpreted as a three-course meal.

Selecting your event caterer

Choosing a caterer takes time. You have to find, shortlist, and interview and select them. You may, of course, have to use the venue's caterers, but be no less diligent in your dealings with them.

A word to the wise

If you are using the venue or your in-house catering, do you believe they are genuinely up to the job? Will they be able to cope and provide the level of service or quality of food you require? So:

- Always arrange to meet your preferred caterer to discuss your menu options, possible layout options, maximum capacities, food preparation and serving options
- Ensure you agree with your caterer the ratio of serving staff to guests

- It is now common for about 25% to 30% of your audiences to have special dietary needs, so build choice into your event catering
- Try to establish whether your food is going to be prepared on site or off site and then finished at the venue. Where will the finishing take place?
- If you are using external caterers, do make sure they check to ensure that their trays and serving platters fit into the venue's ovens
- You may want to consider whether you provide any food for your event staff, perhaps in another room
- Having agreed overall numbers, you must agree with the caterer when final numbers need confirming (usually a few days before event day)
- Get everything in writing and in a contract

Top tip

One of the most common and overlooked catering issues is that event planners need to understand how their guests will eat the food provided, which is not as daft as it sounds. If you are providing food that needs to be eaten with a knife and fork, everyone will need somewhere to sit and, ideally, a table to sit at. If you do not have the room or the tables and chairs, change your food offering to a sandwich buffet, bowl food or finger food.

Mobile catering at outdoor events

If you intend to book a mobile catering unit for an outdoor event such as a team building, family fun day or community project, you will need to consider the following:

- Times you will allow them on site
- Trading times—opening and closing times
- Permitted delivery times

- Location and size of pitch required
- Insurance policies to cover the units and towing vehicles
- Food hygiene certificates
- Local authority registration details
- Access to drinking water
- Rubbish clearance
- Staffing levels and dress code
- The need to carry appropriate fire-fighting equipment at all times

How to get people back after the break

Your event will be punctuated by a series of breaks. Getting delegates back from the break, however, requires strategy. Depending on the size of your event and venue, you can:

- Use volunteers to move through the audience asking them to return to the next session
- Use flashing lights or music
- Ring a bell and shout loudly
- Make sequenced announcements similar to those in a theatre. for example "tonight's show will commence in 10 minutes, so please make your way to your seats"

In summary

- The programme is the main reason why audiences attend events. It is often the determining factor in establishing whether your event has been a success in the minds of your audience.
- It takes time, effort and money to put together a great event programme. It does not have to cost a lot, but it does help to have a realistic budget in place, given the importance of getting this part of your event right.

- For certain events, do make sure your programme provides those "light bulb moments", the game changers. If not, people may vote with their feet and wonder why you do not just post them the video.
- Always do your research. Find out what works, and be brave enough to seek out new things for your audience to experience.
- If you run annual events, be prepared to try something different each year. Programmes must grow and develop. Items that have worked well in the past will not always work well in the future, so be prepared to replace or rethink old programme items that no longer excite the audience.
- Think "theatre", think "show", think "performance", and think "presence on stage" and not just "seniority".
- The room needs to be buzzing, so how are you going to create energy in the room
- Do make sure you do everything in your power to run the advertised programme on schedule.
- Try to make sure wherever you can that your programme contains "people stories"—success stories from people who understand the audience's worlds.
- Think "legacy". How are you going to keep the event's buzz going after the show has ended?
- What presentations or recordings are you going to make available to delegates and how?

CHAPTER 7

PROMOTING YOUR EVENT: HOW TO DESIGN EFFECTIVE EVENT PROMOTIONAL CAMPAIGNS

Your event may be the next big thing but, if your event promotion misses the mark, your event will fail.

Great event, poorly promoted = certain failure

The aim of all your promotional activities must be to draw people to your event: to excite them to buy, enquire, email, talk to you, sign up, purchase tickets or to register interest. You must give them a compelling reason to attend, so think more about the benefits of attendance than just giving them the facts.

It is important to use a combination of great words and visuals wherever you can. While you may categorize your organization as operating in the business-to-business or business-to-consumer environment, you are actually operating in the people-to-people market. People are the ones who make all the decisions, so make sure your promotional material reflects this fact—be human and appeal to people's emotional sensibilities.

Event promotional plans

Every event must have a promotional plan. Depending on the size or importance of your event, the plan may be quite a simple affair with few activities or something that contains multiple activities and preparatory tasks.

Here are eight stages you should consider when putting an event promotional plan together:

1. Set some objectives. What is the purpose of your event promotional plan?
2. Do an audit of what promotional media you already have or can access; it would be wise to conduct a SWOT analysis at this stage
3. Decide who your audience is and create an audience profile
4. Create the content and key messages
5. Select what media you are going to use, then cost it
6. Test, check and review your content and plan
7. Implement the plan
8. Monitor each part of the plan to determine what is working, namely delivering the numbers, sign-ups and enquiries

In more general terms, it is wise to also be aware of the following:

1. Do you know exactly who your target audience is? Where do you find them? What are the voices in their head saying? What problems do they have? (Clearly your promotional material and content needs to be speaking to your audience: your niche.)
2. How does your target audience typically find out about events?

3. The more you spend on the event, the greater the risk, the harder you have to work to get people to the event and, therefore, the bigger the promotion budget you need

4. For new events, you may have to spend around 15% to 20% of the total event budget (creative input, graphic design time, print costs, distribution costs, adverts, updates) on promoting it

5. Where you are purely promoting to an existing list of subscribers or members, it is possible to spend little by way of money. However, you have to be persistent. Very few of us actually sign up straightaway and we will need persuading, so offer great incentives. Most of us need from three to seven "touches" before we do anything; some need a lot more

6. Your promotional plan needs time to succeed. We are all busy people with hectic lives, who need time to plan any event visits. I would recommend a 12-week lead-in time. (Delays in getting the word out about your event can be very costly, so ensure deadlines are not missed.)

7. Keep building your list; the more prospects you have on your list the more people you can market your events to, and consider the need to purchase a list of the right people

8. If you know your audience uses social media sites such as Facebook, Twitter, and LinkedIn, it might be beneficial for you to do the same; however, it might be a good idea to take expert advice before running a social media campaign

9. It is important to think beyond a company's own customers in order to draw a large audience—think about with whom you can collaborate. Can you create a joint venture with a non-competing partner? (Support from them usually means getting access to their list,

which adds legitimacy and reach to your promotional activities.)

10. VIP lists—consider if there are any people (such as industry or thought leaders) you really do want to attend, and allow them complimentary passes; their presence will provide kudos and may encourage others to sign up. (You could create "hot seats" at the front for special guests or people you would like to work with.)

11. One technique that can work well is if the company chief executive personally invites 30 people from their contacts list. (For this to work well, the invitation needs to come from the pen or inbox of the chief executive and be name-specific and signed. If it is not, it will look like another letter created on their behalf; worse still, if it is "pp" (signed by somebody else), it certainly will not look like a personal invitation.)

12. Be realistic, not optimistic, about numbers

Promotional media

In essence, there are three types of event promotion:

- Paid-for media—adverts, promotions
- Earned media—coverage earned on the back of your own public relations campaigns
- Owned media—these are your own promotional campaigns

These media can also be referred to as:

- Inbound marketing—earning the attention of others, by providing interesting content, things that people want
- Outbound marketing—buying attention through direct mail, adverts, posters

Your audiences are also a media channel, so it is great to get them talking about your event.

Here are some of the event promotional possibilities available to you:

- Adverts in magazines, newspapers, specialist, parish
- Adverts on radio, TV, be interviewed
- Direct mail, text messages, DVD
- Exhibitions, guides, listings, events diaries
- Press releases, editorials, advertorials
- Open days, seminars
- Personal selling, speeches—a personal message from key individuals
- Speak about your events, networking events
- Money-off coupons, pricing offers
- Save-the-date campaigns
- Public relations, stunts, events, hospitality
- Event web site
- Email, blogs, podcast, social media, mobile phone, newsletters
- Advertising
- Email signature text, live link
- Banners, pop-ups, drops
- Leaflets, stickers, inflatable blimps
- Partnerships—forming mutually beneficial joint ventures and alliances; you could double your reach
- Literature download, "get your free report here"
- Packaging, promotional branding on parcels, packages
- Postcard marketing

Word of mouth

An important point to remember is that the average businessperson will receive hundreds of messages a day. No wonder things are lost or not opened. However, something that will cut through the clutter is our willingness to listen to other people, especially people we know and trust. It is worth considering who can deliver your word-of-mouth event messages. As the event manager you must be the prime advocate of your event. You must be able to transfer the excitement of what you are planning to deliver on event day to prospects and so influence them to buy. Your personal promotional messages need to be just south of arrogant!

Search engines

It is worth pointing out that the vast majority of us look for information using search engines. It therefore pays to make sure your search engine optimisation work means that, if anyone were to type in the name of your event or headline phrase, you would ideally pop up as the top entry in the search results or at least on page one.

Remember that most corporate events do, in fact, have a local audience, so your focus must be on your local contacts and networks. Web sites must be "live", active and regularly updated; then they are more likely to shoot up the search engine rankings.

Events and social media

(NOTE: I am not a social media expert but I know a little about it. As ever, seek advice from experienced professionals who have good reputations in presenting people through social media.)

Using social media will help generate interest in your event but it is not the silver bullet—the deliverer of a full house. Nor is it a substitute for more traditional promotion. It is something you should do alongside other methods—another megaphone to broadcast your message. Its real value is in driving traffic to your event web site, to generate interest.

There are literally hundreds of social media platforms so, if you want event success in this environment, do make sure you know what social media your target audiences are using and who the key players are in that world; you will want them on your side and, ideally, to follow you.

A few too many businesses seem to believe that the online world is the only place to promote their events. True, it is important. But neglect offline event promotion at your peril. Social media is a two-way dialogue, not a one-way sales funnel. Overtly sell and your fans will not love you anymore. You must therefore use a mix of online and offline promotional media.

The overriding success factor remains, as always, that content is king. The essence of good social media content in terms of events revolves around the phrase "who can you help". All the event content you put up therefore needs to reflect this. To increase your visibility on social media platforms aim to create content that incorporates wherever possible text, pictures and a video, or at least two of these.

In terms of what your audience would like to hear about or receive information about, try some of the following:

- Personal insights into behind-the-scenes at festival HQ
- Mentions in the press, with links
- New programme items
- Interviews with the stars of the event
- Pictures of programme activities, entertainment, speakers
- A video of programme activities, entertainment, speakers, venue

- Teaser information
- Special offers
- Surveys, discussions and polls
- Customer feedback and testimonials from previous event delegates

Those who use the various social media platforms effectively post information regularly, seek to open up conversations, share information and gently suggest what action the audience should take next. Each post must link back to your event web site.

Once you start using social media to promote your events, it pays to measure whether all your social efforts are having an effect. Are your audiences now buying tickets, booking places or signing up? Tools like Google Analytics can help you understand what happens on your event web site, such as what links get clicked on the most and what users then do. Do they go on to sign up? In terms of social media, if you cannot measure it, maybe it is not worth doing in the first place.

My final points about social media are:

- It is not free
- It takes up your time
- Your time costs

But in the right hands and for the right events, there is no doubting the power of social media to drive interest in your event.

Generating media interest

Events feature highly in all forms of the press. They are good news stories but will always have to run the gauntlet of being "dropped" to be replaced by the latest local or national news story. However, in order to increase your chances of making it to print, event managers need to work hard to appear on the media radar and, in turn, to generate press coverage. Those who write the stories—the reporters and editors—are generally looking for "people stories", stories with a unique angle, mass appeal and value, things of interest to their readers.

In order to attract the attention of the media, we do, however, have to build relationships with editors and journalists. So how can we get onto the media radar, become news, get people reading about us and get noticed by potential audience members?

Here are a few suggestions:

- Paid-for adverts
- Advertorials
- E-newsletters
- Editorial
- Press conference, launch
- Direct mail
- Advertising (free) on TV, radio, an organizer or artiste interview
- A competition
- Articles, adverts in trade or specialist magazine
- Mail shots to your database
- A mailshot to, or campaign run by, your sponsor to their network

You may want to have an "event media partner". If you do, you may have to buy an advert in return for additional coverage. In this case, you will need to insert words like "Our media partner is XYZ company" in any adverts, web sites or promotional material.

As with all promotional activities, do monitor what happens. You need to know which activity is working, and whether it is delivering sales or enquiries.

How to write a great creative brief and get what you want

You are likely to have to brief a graphic designer, or someone on the team with skills in that area. It is important to take time to think about what will be the best design, copy and messaging for your event. If you get this right, everyone will be happy.

The graphic design brief should cover the following:

- Description of task—complete description of design and copywriting task and the promotional media being used, such as web site, brochure, poster, direct mail campaign
- Event background—any important information is useful about the host organization, what they do, how they do it, as well as any historical data about previous events
- Audience—you must provide them with a very clear idea of the target audience, who they are, what they do, what they like, what they might want to see or read about, so your designer can consider what sort of images will excite or interest them
- Purpose—you need to decide what the principal purpose is of the poster, email and web site, and the design needs to reflect what you want the reader to do
- Timeline—great design and copy takes time to produce; there will be first, second and third drafts, so do ensure you allow plenty of time for the designers to get it right

Writing great event copy: persuading visitors to come

Copywriting is described as salesmanship in print. The words you use to promote your events are there to persuade people to give up their free time, to buy a ticket, to attend. All your promotional activity must be designed to deliver people, otherwise why are you doing it?

Above all, always remember that your event promotional activities must:

- Grab attention—you will need a great headline to encourage people to read on
- Gain interest—show the benefits of attending
- Create desire—through a special offer, a discount and a "book now" action button
- Instigate action—what do you want them to do; email, visit or call you?

One of the techniques that experienced copywriters use is what they call the four Ps approach to persuasion:

- Promise—grabbing attention through "What's in it for me statements?"
- Picture—building benefits using vivid, descriptive language
- Proof—backing up the picture with statistics, testimonials, research, graphs, charts
- Push—the persuasive grand finale, with a call to action

Not surprisingly, the actual words you use on your promotional material play a very important part in delivering customers. There are a number of words that are considered particularly persuasive. They are:

- Discover: evokes feelings of opportunity, suggests a better life
- Easy: it relaxes us and removes apprehension
- Good: evokes stability and security
- Save: everyone likes to save—time, money, trouble
- Guaranteed: we all fear making a mistake, so guarantee the results
- Proven: nobody wants to be a guinea pig for a new product or service; show them proof
- Money: can your product, service or event make or save them money; if so, how much?
- Safe: safety is important to everyone, it makes us feel secure and evokes trust
- New: if it is new, it must be better, it gives you an advantage over your peers
- Results: we like to know that the product or service can deliver measurable and tangible results
- Own: we find buying decisions tough to make; however, owning something is different; thoughts of owning rather than buying transports your customers into the future, invoking feelings of pleasure and safety
- Free: this word has always drawn curiosity; structure your offer to include certain extra "free" items; please do not, however, use the word "free" in your email subject heading
- Freedom: can your product or service deliver freedom to use our time more efficiently, remove repetitive tasks, give us freedom of choice? If you can deliver freedom for your customers, use the word
- Health: if your product or service delivers a healthier life style in some way, tell them
- Best: if something is the best, it stands out from the rest; surely we all deserve the best
- Investment: rather than talk about the price, consider your purchase as an investment; there is a psychological link to a perceived payback, a return on investment

The above words have persuasive powers. Yes, they really do. Consider how you can use them in your promotional material. People also like to know "how to" do things—make money, solve problems, improve, develop . . . So can you incorporate a "how to" into your promotional material?

There are two further points to note here. Firstly, once people have bought a ticket or signed up, you need to continue communicating with them. It is called a "stick" campaign. Strangely, quite a few of us, even if we have gone to the trouble of buying a ticket, still do not turn up. By running a "stick" campaign, reminding people of the event's highlights, you will reduce your event's no-show rate.

Secondly, you need to incentivize ticket sales. Give them an early-bird offer, such as a two-for-one deal or a gift. Why? Because they work.

Note: if, however, you are not a great copywriter, ask someone to look over your copy. They could make a few changes and increase your conversion rate.

Designing an event poster or e-flyer invitation

Event posters need to catch the eye. In this case, less is more. Headline statements need to be in big bold fonts. The message needs to be clear and concise, informative and sincere, and should tell the audience when, where and why they should attend. It should outline booking incentives, explain what to do next and signpost them to more information.

Stick only to the key highlights. You can create links in the text for those who want more information. Do also make sure that any electronic invitations or e-flyers are saved in common file formats, such as .pdf or jpg, and that they carry the logos of any hosts and sponsors.

Creating event web sites

As the vast majority of us now use search engines to find anything out, it is important that you have a web presence, a page on an existing site or, better still, your own event web site. Event web sites can be whatever you want them to be or whatever the budget or your technical know-how allows them to be.

However, if your event is purporting to be a "little special", you clearly need a web site to match. Remember that perception is reality, so everything about your event has to be special, which includes all the promotional material and media you use.

Ideally, your event web site would contain all or most of the following:

- Event name—brief overview
- Day, date, time, capacity
- Sponsors and links
- Pricing policy and offers
- Online ticketing, registration, e-commerce, payment methods, downloadable forms
- Sign up to workshops tools, appointments system
- Social proof—testimonials, photos, videos of past events, statistics
- Video about the event that paints a picture of the event, a mini-commercial
- Top ten reasons to come, to exhibit
- Destination guide—information about the location, things to do, facts about the place; think in terms of a visitor's trip, a day out, local tourism contact

- Venue—detailed description of the venue, such as how to get there by foot, car, bus, train, from all possible directions
- Include maps, car parking details, any charges, walking times to event from car parks, any special arrangements in place for disabled people, coach parties
- Clear navigation channels—if you are thinking of attending, "click here", or exhibiting, "click here"
- Nearby hotels, accommodation and any special offers available to delegates
- Event programme at a glance—speaker, artiste, biography. What will the audience learn? You could also include a 60-second promotional video from each speaker
- Site plan
- Frequently asked questions section
- Attendee and exhibitor lists
- Dress code, if appropriate
- Any social networking links or ways for delegates to connect before or at the event
- Further information contact points—phone number, email address
- Show offers
- Common branding across all promotional media
- A system for adding news items, blogs, programme updates
- Any details of what you will be making available during or after the event, like copies of presentations

When you are starting out, you are not likely to be able to afford all of the above but do try to improve your event web site year on year. Take note of what your audiences are saying and try to deliver a web site that answers all, if not most, of their enquiries.

Capturing some images of your event

Hire or designate somebody to take photographs. Ideally, somebody who actually knows what they are doing and who has an eye for the picture. You must have some lasting images of your event, not only for your records and sponsors but also to share on social media platforms. Digital photography allows event planners to create some great images. These images will often go on to form the basis of next year's event promotion too.

Similarly, you should try to capture some video footage of your event, such as arrivals, networking sessions, workshops and presentations. You should also endeavour to get some guests to do a video testimonial for you at the end of the event. Again, you can use them in your event evaluation and to promote future events.

Setting a ticket or registration price for your event

While it may be possible to provide free "at the point of entry" events, many of you will need to charge an entry fee. As budgets become tighter, a lot more event managers will have to charge an entrance fee. Typically, all free corporate events will have a no-show rate of about 30%.

My personal opinion is that you should charge something for events. People will attach more value to things they have had to pay for. While you may get fewer delegates, they are more likely to turn up and better represent your target audience. These are people who might want to buy your products and services.

If you are going to charge an entrance fee, your first consideration is to decide what your financial strategy is. Do you need to make a profit; if so, how much? Is breaking even acceptable or do you need to spend the allocated event budget?

In terms of your pricing strategy, you have three options:

1. **Revenue-orientated**—charge the highest price that the target audience will pay, or price the event for the mass market so affordability is key
2. **Operations-orientated**—charge cheaper prices at times of low demand and higher prices at times of high demand
3. **Market-orientated**—offer package prices, such as two for the price of one, or add an extra show at a reduced rate with the purchase of a full-price ticket

Once you have decided on your financial and pricing strategy, the next job is set a ticket price. How do you get the price right?

You will need to consider:

- The sum total of everything you are going to spend on the event
- The sum total of all sources of income other than ticket sales
- The value of any sponsorship deals
- The value of any grants secured
- Exhibitor or concession fees
- Programmes sales, adverts
- The sale of merchandise, shop items
- How many people you can actually fit into the event space (do not assume you will sell out, so make sure you give yourself room to manoeuvre)
- Whether you need to break even or make a profit

To price your registration or ticket price, you should:

- Add up your projected sources of income (excluding ticket sales)
- Deduct this figure from your total expenditure figure
- Divide the remaining figure by the number of people you can legally accommodate (occupant capacity) = base level ticket price
- Round it up and add a percentage onto each ticket as your profit margin, on the basis that you may not sell out
- Do a quick market test to see if your audience would pay that fee
- Make an allowance, if you want to do an early-bird incentive offer, for tickets sold at the reduced price
- Bear in mind that the break-even point should be somewhere between 50% and 70% of total available ticket sales

Note: consider whether you need to think about a refund policy. If so, in what circumstances does it apply? Do make sure it is clearly detailed on any web sites, at the registration desks and on booking forms.

Ticket design

If you intend to issue a hard-copy ticket, make sure your ticket design includes:

- Event name and description
- Number and type of guests invited, for example admit one adult, admit one child, family ticket
- Price and level of the ticket (full price, discount and early-bird offer)
- Date and event times

- Venue and address
- Any sponsor logos, organizer details, funders
- Ticket number, section, seat number
- A tear-off section
- Watermarking or design to avoid copying
- Contact details for further information, event web site, telephone number
- Dress code
- Ticketing terms and conditions, if possible, such as refund policy and disclaimer

Note: if you are using an online registration system, it may not be possible to include all of the above ticket design features.

Example of an event ticketing plan

The following is an example of the stages you will need to go through when creating an invitation, for example to a celebratory dinner dance:

- Guest list development—A list, B list
- Invitation design
- Details to designer
- Mailing house booked, staff member and or volunteer briefed
- First review of invitation design
- Second review of design
- Invitation to the printer
- Envelopes, addresses, stamps to mailing house or volunteer(s)
- Invitation posted to guest list A
- VIP passes, invitations posted to guest list A
- RSVP cut-off date to guest list A
- Invitations posted to guest list B
- RSVP cut-off date to guest list B

- VIP passes mailed to guest list B
- Draw up guest list and seating plan

Advanced ticket sales

If you are charging for your events, I would recommend that you provide advanced ticket sales or some sort of pre-event booking procedure. Advanced ticket sales are cash in the bank and a good indicator of how effectively your event promotional activities are working.

If you do wish to sell advanced tickets, try to:

1. Provide your event visitors with a variety of ways in which to buy a ticket—onsite, over the phone, online or through a ticket agency
2. Ensure that, on event day, collecting pre-sold tickets is quick and easy and there is a way of fast-tracking them through the entrance gates

On-the-day ticket sales

It is event day and the delegates are massing, waiting to get their hands on that all-important ticket. As part of your final preparations:

- Check all electronic ticketing and payment systems to make sure they work, before you open the doors
- Brief all ticketing staff about any on-the-day promotions
- Have an appropriate float and access to spare change to restock floats
- Hire in PDQ (portable chip and pin) machines or tills, if necessary, make sure that the wireless connections for the PDQ machines work at your venue and check

the signal strength, and check your merchant account details

- Ensure that you have sufficient facilities and staff for periods of maximum demand
- Ensure that there are regular cash collections from ticket booths
- Consider how you will store your takings, and whether you have access to a safe, night safe or banking for your takings

Checking tickets on event day

After your guests or visitors have bought their tickets:

- Have stewards in place to check tickets and validate them with a stamp or remove a tear-off section
- Agree, if necessary, depending on the nature of the event, how you will allow re-entry into your event; you could use a hand stamp or something similar to identify people when they present themselves again
- Know your numbers—if your event is likely to have people arriving throughout the day, like an exhibition, it is good practice to use a clicker (handheld counter) to count the number of people you have admitted to your event; for accuracy, remember to count people out too

Event registration systems

There is now a wide range of proprietary event registration software available to the event planner. There are tools to help you manage registrations, tabling planning, and hotel bookings—most of the things you will need. They allow you to email your signed-up list and target list, and give important information about how your various promotional campaigns are working.

They can come free, others will charge you a commission per sale (paid events) and some are subscription-based. They will *not*, however, help you create, for example, a great event programme or promotional campaign. They can make parts of your event planning life easier, though, by helping you to complete those tasks that can be very time-consuming, such as registrations.

Anyone who has dealt with event registrations will know just how time-consuming it is, so anything that can reduce the workload is a good thing. They are generally all easy to use and, once set up, will largely run themselves. A word of caution: please do go into the system regularly to make sure your delegates or guests are completing each field in the way you intended. Personal experience tells me that they do not always do this and, in these cases, you will need to contact them directly or amend their registration details. Not everyone will follow what you believe to be fool proof instructions. The consequence of not monitoring the system is that you end up with incorrect delegate information on event day.

Finally, concerning your event promotion:

- Did you do your audience research?
- Did you know who the audience actually were?
- Were you aware of their needs?
- Did you tell them absolutely everything?
- Did you give a reason to reply?
- Was the "proposition" attractive?
- Did you offer an incentive, such as an early booking discount?

Top tip

Before you go to print, always get a number of people to check your work. You will be amazed at some of the obvious mistakes you may miss.

In summary

- Are you sure that all of your event promotional material makes interesting reading?
- Use great visuals wherever you can.
- Do not be afraid to take advantage of all the many free online or offline event directories that exist.
- When you are in creative mode, don't go into editing mode. They are two separate activities.
- Remember accurate representation! Please do not include images or suggestions of things or people that are not going to be at your event; to do so is misleading.
- The most powerful promotional tool in the book is, of course, you the event manager. Deliver your events messages with passion, energy and professionalism. You must be the prime advocate of what you do.
- It is more important to reach the people who count than count the people you reach. Target your promotional activity.
- Do write and follow an event promotion plan. But do not be afraid to be flexible if it is not working and if change is required or new opportunities present themselves.
- Try to measure the success of your promotional activities; a simple question to ask all enquirers is "How did you find out about the event?" With the answers given, just create a simple bar chart for each of your promotional activities. Then you will know which ones are the most successful.
- If you charge a ticket price, just ensure that your event delivers three times the ticket price in valuable content.
- Always consider how you can incentivize ticket sales by offering early-bird discounts and bonuses. Why? Because they work.

- Does all your promotional material have a call to action?
- Ensure that you hire or designate somebody to take photographs or video footage (or both) of your event.
- A word of warning: if you are looking for savings, please be very careful if you are considering cutting promotional activities; the success of your event is entirely dependent upon how good you are at getting the message out there.
- Event promotion is always a long-term commitment that grows and shows a return over time. Start early, monitor what works and always be ready to seize new opportunities to promote your event.
- Never forget that it is people who make buying decisions— relationships, trust, influence and reputation are just as important in the business-to-business world as they are in the business-to-consumer world. It takes time and patience to build a community of interested parties.
- There is no doubting the power of the many social media platforms to generate interest in events. Just make sure that your event's target audience, or enough of them, are enthusiastic users.
- So, do you know which of your event promotional campaigns are delivering people? You need to know this. Monitor the success of your campaigns.

CHAPTER 8

PRODUCTION: MAKING YOUR EVENT HAPPEN

The production stage can be a stressful time as you begin to feel the pressure and the mounting expectation to deliver a great event. You also know time is running out. It often feels like there are not enough hours in the day to get everything done and your event has temporarily taken over your life. Producing an event is like directing a play: it is built, scene by scene.

There is a necessary and logical order to planning an event and getting this right is important. Essentially, you will need to break down your event day into its component parts and work out what needs to happen first, second, third and so on. The best way to manage this stage of your event is to create an event operational plan or function sheet, taking into account the following:

1. Arrival times—event day management team, contractors, event day staffing team, programme activities, the audience and participants. When do you need everyone on site and in what order? (Key to

the success of this stage is the accuracy of the event joining instructions.)

2. Agreeing public opening times—ticketing, registration and admissions. With opening times agreed, you can then work backwards from this time and calculate how long you will need to get everything and everyone in place. (Setting up an event will always take longer than you expect.)

3. Implementing the event site plan—as your various contractors and event team arrive to help you set the site up, do make sure you have your site plan to hand and that everyone is following it. (A copy of the site plan should form part of your operation plan and should be sent to key staff, the venue and any contractors prior to the event.)

Event operational plans

The important thing at this stage of the event production process is to assume nothing and double-check everything. To help you keep track of what needs to happen during set-up, event day and break-down, I would strongly recommend that you write it all down in the form of an event operational plan.

Essentially, this is a sequenced list of tasks to be completed on or before event day and will include the following:

- A full chronological running order of everything that needs to happen, detailing time, location, person responsible
- Team rotas, numbers, roles
- Programme of speakers, demonstrations, acts
- Schedule of estimated arrival and departure times—of staff, contractors, speakers, guests, teams,

- Useful names and telephone numbers—for contractors, speakers, staff, venue manager, others
- All agreed catering requirements—menus, drinks orders, locations, numbers, and so on
- All special instructions about the venue, site, layout, access arrangements, contact numbers, parking, and so on
- Guest lists, delegate lists and their activity choices, if appropriate
- A full site plan with any accompanying notes
- Contingency and any back-up plans
- List of VIPs, arrival times, special conditions, protocols, and so on
- Emergency plans

The following people will need a copy of your operational plan:

- Venue
- Key staff
- Caterers
- Any other key contractors

Phases of the event

Events are built stage by stage. The following will help you understand what happens at each stage of your event's development:

- Build-up—planning venue design, selecting competent workers and contractors, constructing stages, marquees, fencing, and so on
- Load-in—planning the safe delivery and installation of equipment and services to be used at the event, such as stage equipment, lighting, sound systems, tables

- The event—strategies for running your event, including delegate management, transport plans, fire safety, first aid, emergency plans, running your event programme
- Load-out—safe removal of equipment and services
- Break-down—safe removal and dismantling of infrastructure (barriers, stages, marquees), site clean-up and collection of rubbish

Event joining instructions

Your staff, contractors, volunteers, speakers and entertainers must be given full joining instructions. The accuracy of these instructions sent out or detailed on the event web site are vital to the overall smooth set-up and running of your event. The following should all appear in the joining instructions:

- A full postal address and post code of the venue
- Maps to the site, an overview of the route and a very detailed local map containing any significant landmarks and street names
- Details of when you want them to arrive and what they are to do on arrival, for example to call you or to stay in the car park
- Details of the date and time by which they need to be set up
- Details of anything you have agreed to provide for them
- Times of when they can access the site to break down or complete their work
- Whether they require a vehicle or event pass to access the site during set-up and break-down
- Details of how they can access the site during the event. Are you allowing vehicles onto the site once the event has started and, if so, how? Do they need to call

you first before trying to access the site, so you can arrange for one of your event stewards to help them get onto the site safely?

- Details of any site-specific break-down requirements that you may have, for example do exhibitors or contractors need to leave the site as they found it, or do they need to take away their rubbish?

It is also good practice to send them an overview of the event, such as an outline of the programme content, opening and closing times and (if relevant) a flyer, so they know what they are attending and can tell others about it.

A word of warning: it pays to be aware that those people with satnavs may key in a venue's name or postcode, which could lead them to an area designated by you as the officials' and special guests' parking only. Your event car park may actually be at another nearby location, so make this abundantly clear on your instructions

Note: please remember that not everyone will read this information before they set off, so be prepared when certain event visitors try to blame you when they are late! A lot of things that happen at events are not necessarily your fault but they often become your problem.

Contractor, speaker and entertainment arrival requirements

The following list will help you to decide what information you require from each contractor or activity before they arrive on site:

- Full supplier contact details and addresses
- Exact details of the service being provided, contract or purchase order number

- The sort of access requirements that the venue needs—such as access to an unloading area and knowledge of who needs to authorize the use of these areas
- How long it takes them to set up and complete their work
- How much space they need to set up
- Who will be supervising their work whilst on site, including their name and mobile number
- Who will be driving the vehicles to site, including their name and mobile number
- The services they are expecting you to provide for them—such as power, refreshments, fencing, security
- The relevant safety or fire risks associated with the activity during set-up and during the event
- Do they understand what you expect of them during the event?
- Can they provide you with a 24-hour contact point (depending on what they are providing) in case of failure?
- What is the back-up plan should vehicles break down on their way to the site?

Make sure that you have also requested and received the following:

1. All their event risk assessments, safety documents, certificates and insurance details
2. Confirmation that they have received and understand everything you have sent them, such as maps, passes, special conditions

In a nutshell, put everything in writing and post it to them all. In addition, phone them all to make sure that they have received and understood all the information and joining instructions sent to them. This saves a lot of grief on the day. Do not rely solely on email, as you may find out to your cost just how many emails are *not read*.

Briefing your event day staff

Your event day team will often be a mixture of volunteers, paid staff and contractors. All of them require clear guidelines as to what it is that you want them to do. For smaller events, this might be a short staff briefing meeting and some notes containing information such as:

- An introduction, overview of the event
- Roles and responsibilities on site, your staffing family tree (who they report to)
- Expectations of event staff
- Who the other contractors and key people are on site
- Event and venue evacuation procedure
- Event programme
- Site plan
- List of mobile phone numbers or radio channels (or both)

So what do you expect those helping you on event day to do? The following list (also mentioned in the event planning section) will give you an idea of what the typical roles and responsibilities of a volunteer or team member should be on event day:

- Know who is who on site
- Control traffic movements on site, in and out of the car parks
- Carry out fire and no-smoking patrols
- Keep emergency routes and gangways clear at all times
- Deal with enquiries and log any accidents or incidents
- Give advice on the event programme
- Learn the site layout, location of key facilities, entrances, exits, first aid
- Keep an eye out for any overcrowding issues, particularly near entrances and exits
- Monitor the audience and guests

- Be aware of the location of, and be able to use, fire-fighting equipment
- Know what to do in an emergency
- Keep the site clear of litter
- Concentrate on their duties and only leave their post when told to do so
- Wear clothing and a name badge that clearly identifies them as event personnel
- Remain calm and courteous towards members of the public at all times

Your event team may be required to carry out all or some of the above.

You should also create an event day sign-in and sign-out sheet to include their name, mobile phone number and radio call sign or number, if appropriate. It is always useful to know exactly who is on site and when.

Event guests and VIP protocols

You must know the details of all your event guests (if pre-registered) and any VIPs attending your event. Guest lists and details of VIPs and any associated protocols need to be in the hands of those receiving or looking after them upon their arrival, as well as at the front desk or ticket office. I would always suggest you make specific arrangements to meet and greet all VIPs. They should never have to wait in a queue to get into your event. In terms of any VIPs, please make sure you seek the correct advice. In most cases, they will have somebody or a member of staff who can help you understand what is required of you.

At certain types of events such as conferences or workshops, you could also have lists of people who have prbooked workshops or sessions. It is worth ensuring that, even if these workshops are free, preference is given to those who have already signed up rather than to those who have just turned up. It therefore pays to monitor your lists to see exactly who has arrived.

Event day catering schedules

You will by now have met your caterers, agreed the nature of your event day catering and completed all the necessary safety checks previously outlined. It is now wise to create an event day catering schedule clarifying the following:

- Arrival and set-up times
- Presentation style—buffet, serving stations, number of serving staff, choice of linen, crockery and so on
- Menu details and any special requirements
- What you want them to do on arrival at the venue
- Details of confirmed numbers attending or booked

Having this information agreed in advance will ensure a successful event day catering operation.

The ticket office or registration desk

In many cases, the first time your audience gets to experience your organization in person is when they arrive at the ticket office or registration desk. Their first impressions need to be that of a thoroughly professional-looking organization.

Everybody arriving at your ticket office or registration desk wants a quick, simple-to-follow and accurate service. Here are a few pointers:

- Location of ticketing or registration areas—make them easy to see and with plenty of space in front to queue
- Signage—have clear signs or a person (or both) telling people where to buy, register or collect their tickets
- Always arrange "tickets to collect" alphabetically using a surname or company name—whichever you choose is fine, but be consistent and check that your registration forms request the same information
- Have spares of everything and the capacity to create new badges, for those who have forgotten to register or have had their name spelt incorrectly
- Ensure you have a safe supply of power to any machines running from this area and do check that everything works before the gates open
- Have plenty of staff available to run this area—the service needs to be fast and efficient. (For once-only registrations, where everybody is due to arrive between set times, remember that your registration staff can be redeployed to other jobs once this process is complete.)
- Create a useful box of stationery, spare badges, pens, extension cables, tape, paper, tape and so on

Remember: first impressions count. Ensure this area is kept tidy and looks great at all times. Spare boxes, bags and coats can all be hidden under table-clothed desks.

Name badges

I believe name badges are extremely important at most types of corporate events. They allow those in attendance to become more familiar with each other. Knowing to whom you are talking is comforting for that person and can help to encourage and enhance conversation. There are very few types of events when badging guests is not desirable.

I would also strongly recommend that all event staff are badged and, in this case, have a different coloured badge so they can be easily identified. You may want to consider whether your speakers or sponsors require different coloured badges too.

Here are some points to consider:

- Request name information at the time of registration
- Use as good a quality badge as you can afford
- Be sensitive to your guests' attire—badges should not damage clothing
- Brand your badges—with a company or event logo
- Assure legibility—including the first name, surname and company is fine
- Arrange all badges and tickets—with the name facing out (as guests always spot their names long before you do)
- Print all badges off before your event and not on event day
- Recycle—collect badges on departure
- Have spare badges, clips and cards—just as there are always no-shows, there are also always guests who did not make it through the formal registration process
- Hire or buy a label or badging machine(s)

Top tip

Event production is stressful. To make it less so, spend as much time as you have available before your event making sure everyone knows what to do and when to do it. Then you may sleep a little better!

The event risk assessment

The Management of Health and Safety at Work Regulations 1999 required all employers and self-employed people to assess the risks to workers and any others who may be affected by their undertakings. Event managers are required by law to complete an event risk assessment for all their events. The absence of a risk assessment is a clear indication of legal non-compliance and inadequate safety management. You would have no defence in a court of law should it get that far.

An event risk assessment should cover all aspects of the event.

Your risk assessment must cover all reasonable, foreseeable and significant eventualities.

Generic risk assessments are rarely applicable or responsible because events are consumed at the point of production, and what is produced is never identical. This leaves no space for error, particularly when it could cost a guest, volunteer or member of staff their life. There is therefore no room for a general "one size fits all" event risk assessment. Once you have completed your first risk assessment, you will find a lot its content can be transferred to your next event.

In general terms, a risk is the "chance of something unpleasant happening" (UK Government, 2003). The Health and Safety Executive suggests the following definition: "A risk is the likelihood that harm from a particular hazard is realized."

Risk therefore reflects both the likelihood that harm will be caused and its severity.

A hazard is defined as "something with the potential to cause harm" in a biological, chemical, ergonomic, physical, psychosocial, mechanical and safety capacity. Harm is defined as "death, bodily injury and damage to physical or mental health".

Typical hazards at events

The following are some examples of hazards at events:

- Moving vehicles and possible conflict with pedestrians
- Emergency vehicles unable to get on site
- Slips, trips and falls
- Hearing damage from loud music
- Structural collapse, falling items—stages, marquees, PA towers
- Fire—caterers, structures, electrical, gas, cooking oils
- Food poisoning
- Litter left by the public, stallholders and caterers
- Public disorder—crowds, queues, horseplay
- Danger from electrical installations or electrical failure, such as lighting failure
- Weather—too wet, too hot, too windy and the resultant risk, such as dehydration
- Arena acts—depending on the act
- Other attractions, entertainers, stalls, inflatables, simulators
- Medical emergency
- Fairground, bouncy castle, other attractions—accidents, mechanical failures
- Special effects, fireworks, laser shows
- Alcohol and drugs, and their effects
- Health and hygiene—toilets, washing facilities
- Noise—too loud for staff or neighbours
- Manual handling
- Working at heights
- Lost children
- Barrier fencing failure

- Incorrectly supervised or managed games or activities
- Hazardous substances (COSHH)
- Terrorist attack

So what is a risk assessment?

"A risk assessment is simply a careful examination of what, in your workplace (event), could cause harm to people, so that you can weigh up whether you have taken enough precautions or should do more to prevent harm." (HSE, 2006)

How do you write an event risk assessment?

I would recommend the following 7-step approach:

- Look for significant, reasonable, foreseeable hazards
- Decide who might be harmed and how: rate the likelihood and impact
- Evaluate risk and decide if existing precautions are good enough
- Record findings
- Review and decide if further actions are required
- Implement and decide who will make it happen and when
- Monitor, review and revise these actions, if necessary

There is no right or wrong way to carry out a risk assessment. The law just says you must produce one. While they can be completed in a number of different formats, they all require you to assess a risk, so can be a little subjective at times. There are those that ask you to rate the risk as low, medium and high, while others use a matrix system (using numbers). Either way, the law requires a "competent" person to undertake it.

If you are not sure on any of the above, please seek appropriate advice. I would also suggest that you allow other key personnel to comment on your risk assessment, just in case you have missed something. Your organization may actually already have a set procedure for completing risk assessments, so do check before you create your own.

The dynamic nature of events means that event managers must continually assess risk before, during and after the event. They may therefore need to enforce any necessary control measures on the on-site contractors, security teams and management teams as required. Your risk assessment is not, therefore, necessarily final and may need updating during your event. Be sure to make a note of any event day changes in the event logbook or on the risk assessment.

See Appendix 9 for a sample risk assessment.

Event fire risk assessment

The Regulatory Reform (Fire Safety UK) Order 2005 also required event organizers to write a fire risk assessment. This can be a separate document or be incorporated in the main risk assessment. The format for completing a fire risk assessment is set out below:

1. Identify fire hazards:
   a. Sources of ignition
   b. Sources of fuel
   c. Sources of oxygen
2. Identify people at risk
3. Evaluate, remove, reduce and protect from fire
4. Record, plan, inform, instruct and train
5. Review

There are two HM (UK) Government guides about fire safety, which you may find useful. They are:

1. Fire Safety Risk Assessment—small and medium places of assembly
2. Fire Safety Risk Assessment—open air events and venues

Emergency event planning

Accidents, incidents and emergencies of every type can happen at events. The consequences of such occurrences can range from the catastrophic to the unfortunate, and everything in between. It is always necessary for event managers to plan for such things.

Note: if you are hiring an indoor venue, the emergency planning responsibilities lie with the venue. *However,* you and your event day staff must be aware of the venue's procedures, as you will be part of the solution. So please read on, as this information is still important to you and there will be occasions in your event planning career when you will need to create your own emergency evacuation plans.

Here are some examples of the types of emergency you could face at an event:

- Small-scale incident—requiring local enforcement and procedures
- Fire—bins, catering unit, electrical units and connections
- Medical emergency—minor through to major incidents (multiple casualties)
- Crowd disturbance
- Suspicious packages, bomb threat
- Structural collapse

All of the above can, and do, happen at events of all types and sizes. Please ensure that you plan accordingly.

Event control centre

In the event of an emergency, it is usual for event control (in a room, area or cabin) to become the emergency meeting point. The safe use of this area would depend upon where the emergency was taking place on the site. It is likely that, if a major emergency occurred, the situation would require a multi-agency approach in which the event managers, police, ambulance and fire services and stewards would all play a part. This is why they need a place to meet to discuss their plan of action.

Managing an emergency

The following will give you some pointers as to how you can plan to deal with an emergency.

Declaring a crisis

Any of the following possible occurrences or a combination of them may trigger the need to consider declaring a crisis:

- First-hand witness statements of the incident
- An on-site report by any member of the event team, contractors or member of the public
- A report or comment received from an external source suggesting there is a situation occurring

Verification of the situation

As soon as the event manager or any members of the event team become aware of the situation, they must try to verify the reports immediately. The following questions will help to assess the situation and your response to it:

- What has happened or could happen?
- Where did it, or will it, happen?
- When did it, or will it, happen?
- Why did it, or will it, happen?
- Who is, or will be, affected?
- Was anybody injured or killed, or what is the potential for injury or death?
- What has already been done to control the situation?
- Is there any remaining danger?
- Has anybody been notified?
- Have the authorities or emergency services issued any advice in relation to the situation, such as weather warnings?
- Is there any structural damage to the building or infrastructure on the event site?
- Have any part of the facilities or events operations been interrupted?

Assessment

At this point, you will need to assess the severity of the crisis. Consider whether it is a:

- Local incident, which can be dealt within existing operational procedures
- Major incident or situation, which needs to be declared as an emergency and for which the appropriate services need to be called

Implementing an emergency evacuation plan

It may be necessary to evacuate your event site, so your emergency plan will need to consider the following:

- Identification of key decision-making personnel
- How you can STOP the event's proceedings with immediate effect
- Details of any coded messages to alert event managers and stewards
- Details of any public announcements to be made to the audience and who will be responsible for their delivery
- Identification of rendezvous points for emergency services—where they can meet and park their vehicles
- An outline of what those who will assist you in the evacuation of the site will do, such as opening exit gates, keeping certain areas clear, cordoning-off an area, preventing entry or re-entry
- How you intend to temporarily close down entry systems, to prevent any more people entering the site
- Identification of safe places, where the audience can stand far enough away from the site of the incident

I recommend that the event manager is responsible for making all public emergency announcements and will read from a prepared script where possible. If it is your building or you are hiring a venue, it is likely that an emergency evacuation procedure will already exist. Your job as event manager is to understand it, make your stewards aware of it and work alongside the venue to help them implement the plan.

Small-scale incident

In the case of a small-scale incident at your event, it is likely that you will be able to deal with it locally and with the existing on-site team. You may require your event stewards to undertake some or all of the following actions under the direction of the event manager.

So, upon hearing the message, all event stewards and members of your event team will:

- Stand by to evacuate or cordon-off an area or receive further information (or both)
- Stand by to stop performances
- Move to the emergency exits gates and ensure that there are no vehicle movements on or off the site
- Switch all radios to channel one and maintain radio silence
- Listen to announcements and wait for further instruction—if the incident has been brought to a successful resolution, a "stand down" message should be sent to all stewards via two-way radios, over the public address system or by word of mouth

Major incidents

A major incident at an event is an emergency that requires the implementation of special arrangements by one or more of the emergency services in order to:

- Rescue, treat and transport a large number of casualties
- Handle a large number of enquiries from the public or news media (or both)

In the case of a major incident, the emergency services will follow their own individual procedures. However, the police will normally be responsible for co-ordinating the overall response to a major incident and (if needed) evacuation. The fire brigade will be responsible for all matters concerning fire and rescue, and the medical services for providing emergency treatment and transporting individuals to hospital.

Your event stewards will be asked to undertake some or all of the duties outlined above. Similarly, once the incident has been brought to a successful resolution, and the police concur, you should send a message to your stewards informing them that they can now "stand down". In some circumstances, the event management team may, if necessary, initiate an evacuation without police assistance.

Communicating with your event team

You must consider how you can keep in contact with your event team during your event and not just in an emergency. Multi-channel two-way radios are the best method of ensuring this, and are inexpensive and highly effective. For small events, mobile phones can also be useful. Where possible, all key team members should have a radio. A word of warning: it is always wise to request ear pieces, and use them, so only you (and not everyone around you) can hear what is going on. This is particularly important in an emergency.

An event public address system is also very helpful for passing on key public announcements in difficult situations. If all forms of communication breakdown, having a loud hailer as a back-up is also wise.

Coded announcements

If discretion is required and you do not wish to panic the public, a standard series of coded announcements can be used. Examples include:

- in the event of *fire*, "Would Mr *Ash* please go to . . ." (followed by the relevant area)
- in the event of a *crowd-related disturbance*, "Would Mr *Tyson* please go to . . ." (followed by the relevant area)

- if *first aid* is required, "Would Mr *Nightingale* please go to . . ." (followed by the relevant area)
- in the event of a *major incident*, "Would Mr *Major* please go to . . ." (followed by the relevant area)

Stopping the event

If the situation escalates to a full-scale evacuation of the site(s), the following message will need to be broadcast by the event manager:

> *"Ladies and gentlemen, due to circumstances beyond our control, we must ask you to evacuate the area by walking to any available exit around the venue as quickly and quietly as possible, taking all personal belongings with you".*

A copy of the announcement needs to remain in event control.

Dealing with a fire

In the event of fire that cannot be put out immediately and safely using the on-site fire-fighting equipment, the event manager should contact the emergency services. The event manager will then give permission to clear the area as quickly as possible without causing alarm.

First aid—medical emergency

In the event that first aid is required, the event team should contact the first aid providers (supplied by the venue or you). If a serious incident occurs, or the incident has been caused by something directly related to the event, the event manager must also been informed.

Suspicious packages

In the event of a suspicious package being reported, ensure all event stewards contact the event manager immediately. You should request at this point that stewards do not cause unnecessary alarm. I would recommend the following procedure:

- Over the course of the event, do make announcements reminding the public not to leave belongings unattended
- All event stewards and security personnel must be asked to be aware of what is going on around them and be vigilant
- In particular, remind stewards that, if they see somebody putting a bag down and then walking away from it, they must ask the person to pick it up immediately (it is most likely to be an innocent mistake)

In terms of suspicious packages, stewards should consider:

- Should the item be there?
- Can it be accounted for?
- Is it out of place?

In the event of suspicious items being found, follow this procedure:

5 Cs:

- **Confirm** how long it has been there, whether anyone has been seen with it, whether it has been moved
- **Clear** the area immediately
- **Cordon-off** the area
- **Control** the cordon effectively
- **Check** for secondary hazards or devices

5 Ws:

- **What** the item is, describe it, its size and other features
- **Where** the item is, its exact location and any access route
- **When** the item was found, and whether it has been moved
- **Why** the item is suspicious
- **Who** found it, who the targets are, who the witnesses are

It is equally important that you remind your event team to be aware of what is going on around them. A lot of things can be prevented from escalating into a full-scale incident simply by the event stewards remaining vigilant.

After evacuation

Once the evacuation has been completed, the site will need to be secured to prevent re-entry. Use event stewards or security personnel (or both) for this, and make sure they remain in place until the emergency is deemed to have been brought to a successful conclusion.

The role of the event manager in an emergency

The role of the event manager is to:

- prevent the emergency escalating
- communicate swiftly, effectively and accurately with all key staff
- have an emergency plan or be aware of the venue's procedures (or both)

Event evaluation

You need to find out what everyone actually thought of your event. Evaluating your event is all about expectation versus reality. Did your event deliver what you promised it would? In order to capture this data on event day, you will need to consider, *before* event day, what you want to know and how you are going to capture this information.

Typically, an event evaluation would be looking at some or all of the following areas:

- Customers—guest, participant, sponsor feedback, such as a survey or anecdotal evidence
- Finance—over or under budget, comparison with last year
- Cost effectiveness—did you make smart purchasing decisions, and consider price versus reward?
- Quality—measuring extremes, such as "loved it" or "hated it" and everything in between
- Attendance—was it up, down or the same, and were there any mitigating factors, like the weather or other events nearby?
- Exhibitor, sponsor, partner feedback—was the event a success for them and, if so, why?
- Use of resources—did you use everything at your disposal in the best possible way?
- Deadlines—how many deadlines did you meet or miss, and are there any known reasons why they were missed?
- Social inclusion—did you attract the audience you expected, and was anybody excluded because of how you set up the event?
- Staff morale—did a lack of numbers or resources affect staff at any point during the day?

- The venue—how did the venue's facilities and staff stand up to the task, and were there any delays, breakdowns or other issues relating to how the venue coped on event day?

What you are trying to do is not only evaluate the event (which most of us do) but also evaluate the whole event planning process from conception to completion.

Note: the lessons learnt from one event *must* be incorporated into the planning for the next.

Measuring the success of your event

If you want to secure next year's events budget, you need to know the figures! What was your return on the event? How did you do? What effect has the event had? Did it meet your objectives, such as raising awareness or increasing sign-up rates?

The following will help you measure your *return on objective* figure (*about* the event) and is more about the financial success of your event:

- Know what your total event costs were (all of them) minus all sources of income
- Did you make a loss, a profit or break even?
- Take time to look through the figures and work out where all your income came from—such as ticket sales, shop sales, stands and registrations fees. When you know how your event income was generated, you can make an honest assessment of what did or did not make you any money. (Always consider effort versus reward.)

- Consider any other key external influences such as national and local trends, which may have had an effect your figures.
- Determine what is going to be your measure of success—the money, number of new sign-ups, meetings requested. (This figure ideally would be one of your original event objectives set early on in the event planning stages.)

Measuring your *return on event* figure (the *effect* of your event, which is actually more important than knowing *about* your event) is not a simple task. Most corporate events should deliver value. The only real way to generate value is through the actions of the delegates, so your event must change or reinforce your audience's behaviour.

Event planners therefore need to decide what action they want the audience to take as a result of being at the event. You therefore need to agree:

- What they must learn or experience to change their behaviour
- Who you need in the room, who can learn the most, who you can influence to make the required change
- Whether you have created a good learning environment—including good speaker quality, room layout, temperature and instructions, and whether the audience got to try it out, see it working and hear success stories
- Whether the event fulfilled the audience's expectations, what did they learn or remember, what changed their attitude to you or the situation, what will they do differently now as a result of being at your event
- How you will collect the information—for example, by self-reporting at the event (on paper, on the web, by email or a test) or after the event, or you could check

at a later date to see if they did what they said they would

Measuring your return on event is not easy but, in order to justify next year's event budget, you just may need to know the facts.

A note to follow up after an event

Ultimately the success of most corporate events, where the objective is to create a favourable impression and hopefully encourage prospects to buy from you when they are ready, revolves around your follow-up plan. Hot leads go cold within days.

Your follow-up plan must start directly after the event with a "thank you" email summarising the offer. You would also ask if it you could contact them to get their feedback on whether the event was a success for them. At this point, if they say yes, enquire as to when would be a good time to call. In other words, be expected and, importantly, have some idea about what you want to ask about. Use the above as a guide. During the call, do not try to sell; just listen, advise and help them decide if your services and products are right for them.

Remember: the more follow-up you do, the more successful you will be.

In summary

- Event production requires you to have a very clear idea about what should happen and when. Always attend to the detail—it really does matter.
- Constantly seek to understand how things work.
- Assume nothing; double-check everything!

- You can never put too much information in your joining instructions.
- Constantly talk to everyone, and know what is happening at every minute of your event build, event day and break-down.
- Are you confident that your risk assessment has covered all known hazards and that you have put in place a suitable set of actions to reduce the hazard to an acceptable level?
- Do you know what you would do in a variety of emergency situations?
- Event evaluation is not just a process to be undertaken after your event has finished. Do periodically evaluate how your planning process is going. Are you taking smart decisions, using the budget wisely and sticking to the project plan?
- Fundamentally what you are looking for is a personal recommendation from an event attendee. Would they recommend this event to a friend or colleague?
- Always have a follow-up strategy. If you do not contact people, they cannot say *yes*.

CHAPTER 9

PEOPLE: IT'S BEEN A GREAT DAY

You have now completed all your research, planning, promotion, venue evaluation, programming, procurement, and contracting and event production. The successful conclusion of your event is likely to have been a team effort, driven forward by you, the event manager. How you perform as the event manager during the build-up to event day and on the day itself will be a crucial factor in ensuring the day is memorable for all the right reasons.

The role of event manager

The role of the event manager at this stage is twofold:

- Role 1 is all about the managing the practicalities of running an event
- Role 2 is all about managing your various event teams

Role 1—running the event

The event manager's event day role will require you to:

- Keep control—always agree in advance exactly what you (the organizer(s)) and your contractors are responsible for; create a management structure with reporting lines
- Cooperate—work together, exchanging information; jointly evaluate on-going risks
- Keep in touch with everyone—and update them when necessary
- Monitor safety performance—active monitoring, with inspections of contractors and staff safety methods and comparing these with actual work on site; or reactive monitoring, with actions triggered after an incident, such as reporting injuries, damage and weaknesses in safety standards
- Employ (if required) a safety coordinator—to help you maintain, apply and coordinate a site safety plan
- Engage or coerce competent people—getting expert, experienced, trained or specialist contractors and volunteers on your event team

Role 2—managing your various event teams

On event day, great event managers demonstrate many of the following traits:

Being an inspirational leader who guides, supports, motivates and delivers

Encouraging teamwork, as one of the greatest challenges facing any event manager is creating a real sense of team amongst an often-disparate group of people; the team needs a great team spirit and a strong desire to deliver a successful event

Fostering effective two-way communication, which makes your event team feel involved, valued and committed to the cause

Setting the direction and communicating it with passion, energy and belief, in other words it is the "talking it up" by the event manager that inspires staff to follow and make a commitment

Walking the talk because great event managers lead by example

Making it fun because we do best what we most enjoy

Building trust by letting your staff know where they stand and by being open, honest and above board

Setting high standards in values such as honesty, confidence, hard work, a positive attitude, the ability to praise and inspire, determination, a caring attitude, openness and timekeeping

Promoting creativity and innovation and supporting staff when they make mistakes, because this keeps the ideas coming and gives them the confidence to try new things

Being on hand to seek out and resolve problems, which means always being there for your staff

Making difficult decisions, which is, after all, why you are the event manager; you will also need to understand the art of compromise, because you will need it throughout the event planning process, and you will find yourself having to face up to a few difficult or uncomfortable situations—these come with the job

Appreciating and recognizing the work of your event team, remembering that saying "thank you" is the most underused motivational tool in the book—use it lots!

Involving your event team in everything, because your team members need to understand what you are trying to achieve, why you are doing it and what part they will play

Top tip

Always do unto others as you would have them do unto you.

It's event day

Today is the day—the culmination of all those meetings, conversations, debates, phone calls and emails. It is show time! So, as the event manager, pitch up nice and early and be ready to:

- Know what needs to happen and when
- Observe and listen to everything that goes on
- Advise, guide and manage the set-up
- Solve problems and make quick decisions
- Implement and monitor the event safety plans and risk assessments
- Keep communicating, talking to everyone
- Help and inform event visitors
- Calm and diffuse difficult situations
- Keep control

- Conduct press interviews
- Run the programme to time
- Keep visitors safe—actively monitor how the site is being used
- Lead and manage your event teams

And, of course, to . . . deliver an outstanding event!

Quick reminder

Here are some of the key points discussed in previous chapters to help you create the perfect event.

- Make sure your external team members and your contractors are established suppliers with experience, expertise and exceptional reputations. Please do not be afraid to ask their advice.
- Choose the best venue you can. It is part of the experience.
- Ensure your front-of-house operation is very welcoming: a warm, friendly welcome is vital. A smile and first impressions count.
- Where you can, use lighting (uplighters, colour washes, patterns and projected logos) as they help to set the mood.
- Spend time, effort and money on creating the best, most exciting and most engaging programme you can—with the occasional break for guests to catch their breath.
- Use music that suits all tastes to create atmosphere.
- Plan your site so everyone has room to move, to be served and to be able to see all the action.
- Although you will never please everyone every time, plan the food and drink aspects of your event as carefully and thoughtfully as you can.
- A great master of ceremonies can really bring your event to life. Go for experience and reputation.

- Dress your tables and venue: think candles, flowers, table centres, props, coloured linen . . .
- Make sure all members of your event day team have the right attitude; you can teach them the rest.
- Always say "thank you" to departing guests in person or with a bespoke gift (or both).

In summary

- Select your event team and contractors with care. The success of your event could depend on how well you all work together.
- When giving your event team jobs to do, remember the old adage that people do best what they most enjoy. Match people's talents to jobs.
- On event day, be confident, flexible, aware, motivational and happy.
- Do remember that there is only one thing more infectious than enthusiasm and that is the lack of it—be "up" for your event.
- You cannot spend too much time planning an event. I can assure you that every minute spent on your event is time *well* spent.
- Events are designed, planned and delivered by people for people. You may consider that yours is a business-to-business or business-to-consumer operation but *people* are at the heart of both of these sectors. In reality, your sector is best described as people-to-people. People buy from people; people make the decisions. Keep them at the heart of everything you do.
- Things will happen at your events! People forget things; they do silly things. Sometimes, it will not be your fault but it will certainly be your problem.
- All of us can be great event managers but you will need to fight the battles and learn by doing.

CHAPTER 10

CONCLUSION

Everybody loves a great event, so we need people like you to stand up and say "I will organize this event". Without the efforts of event managers throughout the world, all of our lives would be much poorer. Events are important, unique, complex and planned but, above all else, they are possible.

An event is *live* and therein lies the problem. You will not be afforded the luxury of a full run-through. There are no second chances. With event audiences always expecting the best, organizing a high-quality event experience packed full of great takeaway memories will be no easy task. But if you like a challenge and you have a good dose of self-believe and a determination to succeed combined with good organizational and people skills and you are not afraid to seek advice or ask for help, events are definitely for you.

I would also suggest you always get involved in events that you passionately believe in. Then you will do everything you can to deliver a successful occasion for everyone (including yourself!). Whether you are planning your first event or have been creating them for a while, do follow the 8-Step event planning process outlined in this book. It is the same process that I use every day to organize my clients' events. By doing this, you can be sure that you and your team are always focusing on today's priorities.

So, there you have it. This book has given you the "how to" of organizing successful corporate events. All that remains for me to say is good luck and my final pieces of advice are: keep learning, listening and asking good questions and if you ever need any further help please do call, email, connect or follow me (contact details below). I would love to help. Now it is over to you; it is time to get down to business and deliver those fantastic conferences, launches, meetings, seminars, team building events, exhibitions, dinners, awards—all packed full of great takeaway memories!

Enjoy and good luck!

Chris
Chris Powell
01256 335192
www.theeventexpert.co.uk

APPENDICES

PRACTICAL EXAMPLES, TEMPLATES AND FORMS

Appendix 1: Simple conference budget

This is an example of a very simple budget for a one-day conference.

	Income £	Expenditure £
100 delegates @ £450 per head	45,000	
Sponsorship	2,000	
Total income	**47,000**	
Expenditure		
Staff travel, subsistence, accommodation		1,000
Design, print, stationery		3,000
Postage		2,000
Insurance		300
Stage set		800
Audiovisual equipment		2,000
Delegate packs, information		500
Conference reports, CDs		500
Name badges		100
Venue hire		1,200
Catering @ £40 per head		4,000
Speakers' fees		2,000
Marketing costs (15% of total expenditure)		2,800 (approx.)
Total expenditure		**21,400**
Surplus	**25,600**	

Appendix 2: Detailed event budget

This is an example of a much more detailed budget, which you can tailor to suit your own events.

Conference Budget		
ITEM	**Income £**	**Expenditure £**
INCOME		
Delegate fees @ £ per head		
Sponsorship	:	
Exhibition, display space @ £ per space	:	
Donations	:	
Dinner tickets @ £ per head	:	
Information pack inserts	:	
Total income	**£ :**	
Expenditure		
Staff travel, subsistence, accommodation		:
Printing, stationery		:
Postage, photocopying		:
Insurance		:
Stage set		:
Audiovisual equipment		:
Translation equipment		:
Conference reports, CDs		:
Special needs equipment (such as loop system, signer)		:
Delegate information packs		:
Name badges		:
Venue hire		:
Refreshments, lunches @ £ per head		:
Chairs' fees, speakers' fees, expenses		:
Design, artwork		:
Marketing, promotion		:
Evening meal, conference dinner, wine etc.		:
Toastmaster fees		:
After-dinner speaker fees		:

Entertainment, licences				:
Awards, prizes, gifts				:
Transport, coaching				:
Study tour fees				:
Security				:
Marquees				:
Total expenditure			£	:
Total income £		:		
Total expenditure £		:		
Total £		:		

Surplus/deficit £	:	
Overhead allocation £	:	

Appendix 3: Venue evaluation checklist

Venue Inspection					
Venue					
Location					
Address					
			Postcode		
Contact name					
Tel no		Fax no			
Email		Web site			
Signature of inspector					
Is the venue easy to find?	YES		NO		
Name and distance of nearest railway					
Nearest tube line and station					
Is car parking available?	YES		NO		
Free or Pay & Display	Free		P & D		
Is there a hotel courtesy coach?	YES		NO		
Is there access for delegates in wheelchairs?	YES		NO		
Are guide dogs for the visually impaired allowed in the venue?	YES		NO		

MEETING ROOMS				
(you will need one form for each breakout/workshop/session room)				
Name of room				
Is the lighting natural or artificial?				
Are emergency exit instructions available?	YES		NO	
Is there likely to be any noise either inside or outside the building, such as from the kitchens or from external refurbishment work?				
Draw a basic picture of the room including power sockets, emergency exits, etc.	Picture:			
Are there any pillars or columns?	YES		NO	
Are there any mirrors?	YES		NO	
Are there any windows?	YES		NO	
Is there a blackout facility and, if so, is this adequate?	YES		NO	
Is the room partitioned?	YES		NO	
Is the partition soundproofed?	YES		NO	
Is staging available?	YES		NO	
If so, what size is the staging?				
Is there a cost for the staging?	YES		NO	
Is a lectern available?	YES		NO	
If so, is there a charge for the lectern?	£			
What is the maximum capacity of the room in the following style of layouts?				
Theatre				
Classroom				
U-shape				
Boardroom				
Banquet				
Herringbone				
Horseshoe				
Is it possible for you to see the room in use?	YES		NO	

EQUIPMENT					
Is the following equipment available?					
Public address (PA) system	YES		NO		
Loop hearing system (if yes, where?)	YES		NO		
Is there space for back projection?	YES		NO		
Is there a facility to record the proceedings?	YES		NO		
Is there a technician available on site?	YES		NO		
Name of venue's preferred contractors, if any					
Costs charged by preferred contractors are					
Where is the lights control box?					
Can lights be dimmed?	YES		NO		
Heating system—is it noisy?	YES		NO		
Air conditioning—is it noisy?	YES		NO		
Is the seating comfortable?	YES		NO		
If seating is not comfortable, what can be done about it?					

CATERING	
Name of room	
Is it close to or at the same level as meeting room(s)?	
Maximum capacity for a seated meal?	
Maximum capacity for a standing meal?	
What is the suggested table layout?	
What is the maximum number of serving points? (Recommend 2 serving points per 50 delegates)	
Speed of service for sit-down hot or cold lunch?	
Speed of service for standing hot or cold lunch?	

Will a copy of the menu be available in advance?	YES		NO		
Is private dining available?	YES		NO		
Is a cash bar available?	YES		NO		

Other Facilities

Is a conference organizers' office available?	YES		NO		
Is yes, name of room?					
Number and location of toilets					
What is the general standard of cleanliness throughout the venue?					
What local shops are within walking distance (such as pharmacy, news agents, etc.) ?					
Name and telephone number of local taxi company					

BEDROOMS

Number of single rooms available?					
Number of double rooms available?					
Number of twin rooms available?					
Number of suites available?					
Number of rooms suitable for disabled people?					
How many smoking rooms available?					
What is the size of the bedroom and bathroom?					
What time can people check in?					
What is checkout time?					
Is there a minibar in the room?	YES		NO		
Is there a hairdryer?	YES		NO		
Is there a trouser press?	YES		NO		
Is tea and coffee available in the room?	YES		NO		
Is a desk or table available in the room?	YES		NO		

Is satellite television available in the room?	YES		NO		
Are the leisure facilities free of charge to residents?	YES		NO		
What might cause noise nuisance?					
Is room service available?	YES		NO		
Is breakfast included in the rate?	YES		NO		
If so, what is the price of breakfast?					
Is there an internet link in bedrooms?	YES		NO		
If not, is there an internet link anywhere in the building?	YES		NO		
If yes, where is it located?					

General

Is additional signage necessary?	YES		NO		
If so, how many signs are needed and where should these be located?					
Can signage, posters, exhibition stands be erected in the venue?					
What method of fixing is allowed?					
Will any refurbishment work be taking place during the conference?	YES		NO		
If yes, when and where?					
Is there good access to all areas for delegates and AV crew (such as lifts, stairs, ramps, etc.)?	YES		NO		
If access is not good, what can be done about it?					

BEFORE YOU LEAVE THE VENUE

Obtain a full list of hire charges for all rooms and facilities		
Obtain a copy of the terms and conditions and the cancellation policy		
Ask for a location map and written travel instructions		

Ask for a hotel brochure	
Obtain a business card of your contact	
Obtain a copy of the venue's emergency evacuation procedures	
Ask for a selection of menus and prices	

Appendix 4: Room layout options

Finding the best layout for your conference can be tricky, especially where the room has a number of fixed features. The content of the programme may also dictate a particular layout requirement.

The following diagram shows the various types of layout you may wish to consider as being most appropriate for your meeting.

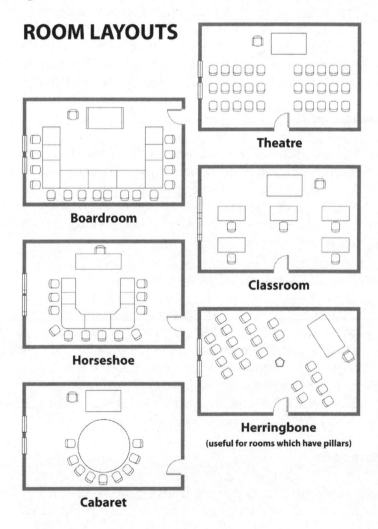

ROOM LAYOUTS

Theatre

Boardroom

Classroom

Horseshoe

Herringbone
(useful for rooms which have pillars)

Cabaret

Guidelines for estimating room capacities

These are rough guidelines only. All room layouts must conform to the venue's fire regulations.

Theatre style

- First row of chairs to be approximately 1.8 metres from the front of the stage (platforms and staging should be at least 30 metres high, even for a small numbers of delegates)
- There needs to be at least 60 centimetres between each row of seats (1.5 metres for wheelchairs)
- Leave a space of 1.2 metres for aisles on each side of the rows of seats as well as in the middle, especially if there are more than 500 people in the audience

Classroom style

- Tables used as desks are usually between 1.8 and 2.4 metres long, and 46 or 76 centimetres wide
- Allow 0.6 metres of table space per person, a little more if using computers
- Allow 90 centimetres between table rows, for wheelchairs allow 1.8 metres

Cabaret or banquet style (round tables)

- Diameters of tables are usually about 152 centimetres (to seat 8 people), 168 centimetres (to seat 9 people) or 183 centimetres (to seat 12 people); wheelchairs require 1.5 times as much space per person
- It is best to leave space between round tables of 1.8 to 2.1 metres for seating and circulation, and to make it easier for food to be served

Remember:

Table measurements can vary from venue to venue.
All layouts must conform to the venue's fire regulations.

Appendix 5: Technical requirements checklist

Many types of venues, although described as "conference centres", are not built for the purpose and this can give rise to a number of problems. This checklist will help you and your production or audiovisual technician to make the best of every venue by giving careful thought and sufficient rehearsal time for conference presentations.

TECHNICAL REQUIREMENTS		
For consideration	**Yes**	**No**
Is the room large enough for back projection? *(To calculate the space required behind your stage set, an approximate gauge is 2.5 times the width of the screen plus 1 metre.)*		
Does the venue have a digital projector?		
Is it in working order?		
Have you tested it well in advance of the presentations?		
Is a television screen available? *(Do not use TV for showing videos if there are more than 30 delegates in the room.)*		
Do you know where to locate the light switches?		
Do you know how to use the light switches?		
Is there a dimmer switch?		
Do you and your technician know how to operate the lights?		
Are there chandeliers in the room?		
Are there any chandeliers casting a shadow over the projection screen?		
If so, can they be removed and what is the cost of removal?		

Does the venue have a domed ceiling? *(This can affect acoustics and create an echo effect.)*		
Does the venue have its own public address system?		
Can it be switched off in the main conference room during sessions?		
Are the blackout facilities effective?		
Use lapel microphones to ensure the speaker's voice is at a constant distance from the microphone *(especially if there are acoustic problems in the room)*		
Is a rehearsal room available?		
Is conference videoing equipment available?		
Are there internet or Wi-Fi connections available? Code(s)?		

Appendix 6: Basic catering schedule

Catering Schedule				
Title of conference				
Date		**Venue**		
Time	**Catering for whom?**	**Type of catering**	**Room/Area**	**Numbers**

Appendix 7: Briefing the chairperson

Choose your chairperson with care. A good chairperson can make the world of difference to a conference, but only if they are well briefed. The following checklist provides a few points to ensure that your chairperson runs the sessions exactly as you require.

Chairperson's Briefing		
Item	**Action (and by whom)**	**Date of briefing**
Provide accurate details on date, time, place and theme		
Provide details of all speakers *(biographies, telephone numbers, email addresses, etc.)*		
Insist that they regularly refer to the theme of the conference to ensure that there is a cohesive programme		
Provide a list of speakers' programme time slots		
Do you require them to hold a question & answer session(s)? If so, at what point in the programme?		
When and where will they meet the speakers?		
What are the hosting arrangements?		
If royalty or a minister is attending, are there any special arrangements or protocol?		
Suggest how the chairperson should deal with the situation if a speaker does not show or is late for their slot		
Encourage the chairperson to make contact with all speakers before the conference		

How long should the welcome, introduction and summing-up by the chairperson take?		
Are there any domestic announcements?		
Will the chairperson take lunch with the speakers?		
Add any other event-specific briefing information		

Appendix 8: Terms of engagement for after-dinner speakers

Name of event:	
Event date:	
Time:	
Venue:	
Name of after-dinner speaker:	
Name of agent (if appropriate):	
Address of agent:	
Contact details:	

1. Introduction

Description of both the nature of company and type of event planned.

2. Delegates

The event attracts between [numbers] delegates who are drawn mainly from [name of sector/industry]. Insert any other relevant information about the audience and the "dos and don'ts".

Delegates comprise [status and profile of delegates].

3. Dinner proceedings

A draft copy of the dinner proceedings is attached. [Add a description of the dinner and the running order, including protocols for those attending (for example a mayor, a politician or international guests).]

4. Dress

State the dress code.

5. Terms

[Example:
Given the mix of delegates (bearing in mind the increasing numbers of females, people from ethnic minorities, people with special needs or disabilities), it must be noted that these delegates are employed by organizations that have strict equal opportunity policies and the after-dinner speaker must remember to be totally politically correct whilst at the same time be entertaining. He/she must avoid telling jokes or anecdotes that are racist or sexist nature or are in any other way offensive or sensitive. This organization [state name of your company] reserves the right to a refund of fees should this condition not be adhered to.]

Signature of after-dinner
speaker / agent and date . . . .

Appendix 9: Sample risk assessment

The following is an example of what you may write for a typical business event.

XYZ BUSINESS EXPO

Date, year, venue

Risk assessment: introduction

The XYZ Business Expo will be held on *date, year,* at *venue.* This is the? time this event has been held. The Expo is organized by ?

The event will be open to the public on date at time. There is *for example* a breakfast seminar in the main auditorium starting at 8.30am. Guests for this event have all pre-registered and number about 50. The event's load-in will start on *date* at *time* with the building of the shell schemes and the installation of the electrical works. The aim of this event is to display 50 of the area's leading businesses. Each exhibitor will be provided with a shell scheme and or space in the ? area of *name of venue.* There will also be 3 seminars taking place in the Conference Room and a keynote speech taking place in the main auditorium.

The event is free to visitors, who will be expected to use the existing network of pay and display car parks when visiting the Expo. We are anticipating an audience of about ? *local business people.*

The following risk assessment will identify the potential hazards and the risks they carry, and will detail the control measures in place to minimize the risk.

Please note that, although this risk assessment was carried out in a systematic manner throughout the site, there may still be hazards that have not been recognized. It is therefore the responsibility of the event team to continually monitor the event for hazards and report them to the event manager immediately.

Completed by:

Name:

Company:

Dated:

HAZARD	CONSEQUENCE IF IT HAPPENS	GROUPS AT RISK	CONTROLS AND ACTIONS	RESIDUAL RISK	PERSON RESPONSIBLE
Access: vehicle movements around the venue	Minor injury, major injury, death	Public, stewards, contractors, exhibitors	Exhibitors and contractors vehicles will be allowed to enter the designated unloading areas at the back of the venue from where they can unload any equipment that needs to be brought to their stand.	Low	Event manager, Expo stewards, The *venue*
Access, egress, exits: emergency vehicles	Minor injury, major injury, death	Public, stewards, exhibitors, contractors	Pre-designated entry and exit routes for emergency vehicles, all exits to be kept clear. In the case of an emergency, Expo stewards will assist with emergency vehicle movements under the direction of *venue* staff.	Low	Event Manager, Expo stewards, The Venue
Car parking: collision with member of the public	Minor injury, major injury, death	Public, stewards, exhibitors	Event visitors will park in the existing network of pay and display car parks. These car parks are either owned or operated by ? or their designated operators. Car park signage and/or management systems are already in place for the safe operation of these car parks.	Low	? Borough Council or designated operator

HAZARD	CONSEQUENCE IF IT HAPPENS	GROUPS AT RISK	CONTROLS AND ACTIONS	RESIDUAL RISK	PERSON RESPONSIBLE
Electrics: fire, electric shock, trip	Minor injury, major injury, death	Public, stewards, exhibitors	Temporary power sockets are going to be installed in each cubicle. Power to these temporary sockets will be drawn from The Lights existing power supply. ? have been contracted to carry out the work. Insurance details and risk assessments have been obtained. Qualified electricians who will carry out all electrical work in accordance with current legislation. Cables will, wherever possible, be located out of the way and, if not, will be covered or flown to avoid trip hazards. A risk assessment has been received from ? contractor.	Low	Event manager, ? contractor

HAZARD	CONSEQUENCE IF IT HAPPENS	GROUPS AT RISK	CONTROLS AND ACTIONS	RESIDUAL RISK	PERSON RESPONSIBLE
Collapse: shell scheme	Minor injury, major injury	Public, stewards, exhibitors, contractors	? are a well-known and reputable shell scheme provider. They will be responsible for the erection of all the shell schemes on the event site, following all the recommended manufacturers' guidelines and their own procedures for erection of such schemes in indoor locations. A method statement and risk assessment have been supplied by ? contractor. The Expo event manager and venue duty manager and stewards will monitor the build throughout the event. The shell schemes will be erected from ? time on ? date and dismantled on the evening of the ? date at ? time. Full address and contact details for ? contractor are as follows:	Low	? Exhibition Company, event manager, Expo stewards

The following are other typical risks at corporate events									
Structures: fire									
Bomb threats									
Litter									
Crowd dynamics: site suitability									
Crowd dynamics: overcrowding, trips									
Crowd dynamics: disturbance									
Catering: food sales, food poisoning									
Emergency evacuation									
Fire									

183

Fire: laptop and plasma screens	Fire: smoking	Electrical appliances	Electrical connections	Emergency exits and gangways	Medical emergency	Health and hygiene	Delegate trips and slips while attending seminars, keynote or other speeches

184

Title of the event: *XYZ Business Expo*

Date:

Venue:

Date risk assessment carried out:

Risk assessment carried out by: *[for example: Name, Event Manager, Company, Contact details]*

Revision: 1

Revision: 2